1-14

D1264190

BERTRAND RUSSELL

NEW HOPES
FOR A
CHANGING WORLD

SIMON AND SCHUSTER · NEW YORK

MANUFACTURED IN THE UNITED STATES OF AMERICA
BY KINGSPORT PRESS, INC., KINGSPORT, TENN.

CONTENTS

PART ONE: MAN AND NATURE

CHAPTER		PAGE
I.	*Current Perplexities*	3
II.	*Three Kinds of Conflict*	12
III.	*Mastery over Physical Nature*	15
IV.	*The Limits of Human Power*	26
V.	*Population*	35

PART TWO: MAN AND MAN

VI. | *Social Units* | 53
VII. | *The Size of Social Units* | 59
VIII. | *The Rule of Force* | 67
IX. | *Law* | 74
X. | *Conflicts of Manners of Life* | 83
XI. | *World Government* | 89
XII. | *Racial Antagonism* | 96
XIII. | *Creeds and Ideologies* | 111
XIV. | *Economic Co-operation and Competition* | 126
XV. | *The Next Half-Century* | 136

PART THREE: MAN AND HIMSELF

XVI. | *Ideas Which Have Become Obsolete* | 147
XVII. | *Fear* | 161
XVIII. | *Fortitude* | 179
XIX. | *Life Without Fear* | 188
XX. | *The Happy Man* | 197
XXI. | *The Happy World* | 206

PART I

Man and Nature

Current Perplexities

THE present time is one in which the prevailing mood is a feeling of impotent perplexity. We see ourselves drifting towards a war that hardly anyone desires—a war that, as we all know, must bring disaster to the great majority of mankind. But like a rabbit fascinated by a snake, we stare at the peril without knowing what to do to avert it. We tell each other horror stories of atom bombs and hydrogen bombs, of cities exterminated, of Russian hordes, of famine and ferocity everywhere. But although our reason tells us we ought to shudder at such a prospect, there is another part of us that enjoys it, and so we have no firm will to avert misfortune, and there is a deep division in our souls between the sane and the insane parts. In quiet times the insane parts can slumber throughout the day and wake only at night. But in times like ours they invade our waking time as well, and all rational thinking becomes pale and divorced from the will. Our lives become balanced on a sharp edge of hypothesis—if there is to be a war one way of life is reasonable; if not, another. To the great majority of mankind such a hypothetical existence is intolerably uncomfortable, and in practice they adopt one hypothesis or the other, but without complete conviction. A youth who finds scholastic education boring will say to himself: "Why bother? I shall be killed in battle before long." A young woman who might live constructively thinks to herself that she had better have a good time while she can since presently she will be raped by Russian soldiery until she dies. Parents wonder whether the sacrifices called for by their children's upbringing are worth while since they are likely to prove futile. Those who are lucky enough to possess capital are apt to spend it on riotous living, since they foresee a catastrophic depreciation in which it would become worthless. In this way uncertainty balks the impulse to every irksome effort, and generates a tone of frivolous misery mistakenly thought to be pleasure, which turns outward and becomes hatred of those who are felt to be its cause. Through this hatred it brings daily nearer the catastrophe which it dreads. The nations seem caught in a tragic fate, as though, like characters in a Greek drama, they were blinded by some offended god. Bewildered by mental fog, they march towards the precipice while they imagine that they are marching away from it.

It must be said that the purely intellectual problems presented by the world of our day are exceedingly difficult. There is not only the great problem: can we defend our Western world without actual war? There are also problems in Asia and problems in Africa and problems in tropical America which cannot be solved within the framework of the traditional political ideas. There are those, it is true, who are quite certain that they can solve these problems by ancient methods. Consider MacArthur and his Republican supporters. So limited is his intelligence and his imagination that he is never puzzled for one moment. All we have to do is to go back to the days of the Opium War. After we have killed a sufficient number of millions of Chinese, the survivors among them will perceive our moral superiority and hail MacArthur as a savior. But let us not be one-sided. Stalin, I should say, is equally simple-minded and equally out of date. He, too, believes that if his

armies could occupy Britain and reduce us all to the economic
level of Soviet peasants and the political level of convicts, we
should hail him as a great deliverer and bless the day when we
were freed from the shackles of democracy. One of the painful
things about our time is that those who feel certainty are stupid,
and those with any imagination and understanding are filled
with doubt and indecision. I do not think this is necessary. I
think there is a view of man and his destiny and his present
troubles which can give certainty and hope together with the
completest understanding of the moods, the despairs, and the
maddening doubts that beset modern men. It is my hope to set
forth such an outlook in the following pages in a way that shall
be convincing and overwhelmingly encouraging, that shall enable men of good will to work with the same vigor which of
late has been the monopoly of cruel bigots; to take away from
our Western mentality the reproach that we have nothing to
offer inspiring the same firm conviction and the same solid
body of belief as is offered by the disciples of the Kremlin.
But I anticipate. And after this digression into hope I must return to the causes of its opposite, which have all too much
sway in the reflections of thoughtful men. If we forget Mac-
Arthur and his simplicities, what are we to think about Asia?
From the time of Vasco da Gama until the Russo-Japanese war,
the Western world did not think seriously about Asia. No
doubt it was a picturesque continent, and amid our progressive
schemes we enjoyed talking about the unchanging East. Philosophers with kindly contempt, and missionaries with reforming zeal, studied what we were pleased to call their
superstitions. We enjoyed their military incompetence, and
their incapacity to extract high wages. For all these reasons
we rather liked them. We realized, of course, that the inhabitants of Asia did not all form one community. There were
Mohammedans and Hindus and Buddhists, and it was our hope
that they would continue to hate each other forever. And on

this ground the more enlightened among administrators depre-
cated the work of missionaries for fear lest it should diminish
the virulence of "superstition."

The first country of Asia to cause misgivings in Europeans
was Japan. At first, after Commodore Perry had opened the
country to our curiosity, we admired the cherry blossom,
Bushido, and the chivalrous virtues of the Samurai. We liked
the temples and the art, and our aesthetes imagined the Japanese to be kindred souls. But gradually a change came over the
spirit of our dream. It may be seen in the works of Lafcadio
Hearn. At first he was enthusiastic about the Japanese, but his
last book, *Japan, an Interpretation*, has begun to be aware of
things slightly more serious than cherry blossom. The Japanese
refused to stay put. They set to work to imitate the West, and
in the measure in which they succeeded they inspired hatred in
Western minds.

The Japanese for the moment encountered disaster; they
mastered our brutalities, but not our suppleness. But they left
to the rest of Asia a legacy of warlike rebellion against Western insolence. Western men of liberal outlook cannot but
sympathize with the wish of Asia to be independent, but it
would be a pity if this sympathy were to blind Western
thought to certain matters of the gravest import. The Western
world has achieved, not completely but to a considerable extent, a way of life having certain merits that are new in human
history. It has nearly eliminated poverty. It has cut down illness and death to a degree that a hundred years ago would
have seemed fantastic. It has spread education throughout the
population, and it has achieved a quite new degree of harmony
between freedom and order. These are not things which Asia,
if it becomes quickly independent, can hope to achieve. We,
in the West, aware of the appalling poverty of Southeast
Asia, and convinced that this poverty is a propaganda weapon
in the hands of the Russians, have begun to think for the first

time that something ought to be done to raise the standard of life in these regions. But their habits and our beliefs between them make the task, for the present, a hopeless one. Every increase of production, instead of raising the standard of life, is quickly swallowed up by an increase in population. Eastern populations do not know how to prevent this, and Western bigots prevent those who understand the problem from spreading the necessary information. What is bad in the West is easily spread: our restlessness, our militarism, our fanaticism, and our ruthless belief in mechanism. But what is best in the West—the spirit of free inquiry, the understanding of the conditions of general prosperity, and emancipation from superstition—these things powerful forces in the West prevent the East from acquiring. So long as this continues, Eastern populations will remain on the verge of destitution, and in proportion as they become powerful, they will become destructive through envy. In this they will, of course, have the help of Russia, unless and until Russia is either defeated or liberalized. For these reasons, a wise policy towards Asia is still to seek.

In Africa the same problems exist, though for the present they are less menacing. Everything done by European administrators to improve the lot of Africans is, at present, totally and utterly futile because of the growth of population. The Africans, not unnaturally, though now mistakenly, attribute their destitution to their exploitation by the white man. If they achieve freedom suddenly before they have men trained in administration and a habit of responsibility, such civilization as white men have brought to Africa will quickly disappear. It is no use for doctrinaire liberals to deny this; there is a standing proof in the island of Haiti.

It must not be supposed that there is any essential stability in a civilized way of life. Consider the regions overrun by the Turks and contrast their condition under the Turks with what they were in Roman days. Over great parts of the earth's surface, similar misfortunes are not impossible in the near future. On the other hand it must be admitted that until we include birth-control in our African policies every increase in efficiency and honesty and scientific skill on the part of European administrators will only increase the sum of human misery.

The population problem is similar in Central and South America, but it does not there have the same political importance.

I have been speaking hitherto of public perplexities, but it is not these alone which trouble the Western mind. Traditional systems of dogma and traditional codes of conduct have not the hold that they formerly had. Men and women are often in genuine doubt as to what is right and what is wrong, and even as to whether right and wrong are anything more than ancient superstitions. When they try to decide such questions for themselves they find them too difficult. They cannot discover any clear purpose that they ought to pursue or any clear principle by which they should be guided. Stable societies may have principles that, to the outsider, seem absurd. But so long as the societies remain stable their principles are subjectively adequate. That is to say they are accepted by almost everybody unquestioningly, and they make the rules of conduct as clear and precise as those of the minuet or the heroic couplet. Modern life, in the West, is not at all like a minuet or a heroic couplet. It is like free verse which only the poet can distinguish from prose. Two great systems of dogma lie in wait for the modern man when his spirit is weary: I mean the system of Rome and the system of Moscow. Neither of these gives scope for the free mind, which is at once the glory and the torment of Western man. It is the torment only because of growing pains. The free man, full grown, shall be full of joy and vigor and mental health, but in the meantime he suffers.

Not only publicly, but privately also, the world has need of ways of thinking and feeling which are adapted to what we know, to what we can believe, and what we feel ourselves compelled to disbelieve. There are ways of feeling that are traditional and that have all the prestige of the past and weighty authority, and that yet are not adapted to the world in which we live, where new techniques have made some new virtues necessary and some old virtues unnecessary. The Hebrew prophets, surrounded by hostile nations, and determined that their race should not be assimilated by Gentile conquerors, developed a fierce doctrine in which the leading conception was sin. The Gentiles sinned always and in all their ways, but the Jews, alas, were only too apt to fall into sin themselves. When they did so they were defeated in battle and had to weep by the waters of Babylon. It is this pattern which has inspired moralists ever since. The virtuous man has been conceived as one who, though continually surrounded by temptation, though passionately prompted to sin, nevertheless, by almost superhuman strength of will, succeeds in walking along the straight and narrow path, looking meanwhile disdainfully to the right and left at those inferior beings who have loitered to pluck flowers by the way. In this conception, virtue is difficult, negative, and arid. It is constrictive and suspicious of happiness. It is persuaded that our natural impulses are bad and that society can only be held together by means of rigid prohibitions. I do not wish to pretend that society can hold together if people murder and steal. What I do say is, that the kind of man whom I should wish to see in the world is one who will have no impulse to murder, who will abstain from murder not because it is prohibited but because his thoughts and feelings carry him away from impulses of destruction. The whole conception of sin has, as it were, gone dead, so far, at least, as conscious thought and feeling are concerned. Most people have not thought out any other system of ethics, and have not, perhaps, theoretically rejected the old system. But it has lost its hold on them. They do not murder or steal as a rule, because it would not be to their interest to do so, but one cannot say as much for their obedience to the Seventh Commandment. They have, in fact, no wish to conform to the ancient pattern. The Publican thanks God that he is not as this Pharisee, and imagines that in so doing he has caught the point of the parable. It does not occur to him that feeling superior is what is reprehended, and that whether it is the Publican or the Pharisee who feels superior is an unimportant detail.

I should wish to persuade those to whom traditional morals have gone dead, and who yet feel the need of some serious purpose over and above momentary pleasure, that there is a way of thinking and feeling which is not difficult for those who have not been trained in its opposite, and which is not one of self-restraint, negation and condemnation. The good life, as I conceive it, is a happy life. I do not mean that if you are good you will be happy; I mean that if you are happy you will be good. Unhappiness is deeply implanted in the souls of most of us. How many people we all know who go through life apparently gay, and who yet are perpetually in search of intoxication whether of the Bacchic kind or some other. The happy man does not desire intoxication. Nor does he envy his neighbor and therefore hate him. He can live the life of impulse like a child, because happiness makes his impulses fruitful and not destructive. There are many men and women who imagine themselves emancipated from the shackles of ancient codes but who, in fact, are emancipated only in the upper layers of their minds. Below these layers lies the sense of guilt crouching like a wild beast waiting for moments of weakness or inattention, and growling venomous angers which rise to the surface in strange distorted forms. Such people have the worst of both worlds. The feeling of guilt makes real happiness impossible for them, but the conscious rejection of old codes of behavior makes them act perpetually in ways that feed the maw of the ancient beast beneath. A way of life cannot be successful so long as it is a mere intellectual conviction. It must be deeply felt, deeply believed, dominant even in dreams. I do not think that the best kind of life is possible in our day for those who, below the level of consciousness, are still obsessed by the load of sin. It is obvious that there are things that had better not be done, but I do not think the best way to avoid the doing of such things is to label them sin and represent them as almost irresistibly attractive. And so I should wish to offer to the world something scarcely to be called an ethic, at any rate in the old acceptation of that word, but something which, nonetheless, will save men from moral perplexity and from remorse and from condemnation of others. What I should put in the place of an ethic in the old sense is encouragement and opportunity for all the impulses that are creative and expansive. I should do everything possible to liberate men from fear, not only conscious fears, but the old imprisoned primeval terrors that we brought with us out of the jungle. I should make it clear, not merely as an intellectual proposition, but as something that the heart spontaneously believes, that it is not by making others suffer that we shall achieve our own happiness, but that happiness and the means to happiness depend upon harmony with other men. When all this is not only understood but deeply felt, it will be easy to live in a way that brings happiness equally to ourselves and to others. If men could think and feel in this way, not only their personal problems, but all the problems of world politics, even the most abstruse and difficult, would melt away. Suddenly, as when the mist dissolves from a mountain top, the landscape would be visible and the way would be clear. It is only necessary to open the doors of our hearts and minds to let the imprisoned demons escape and the beauty of the world take possession.

Three Kinds of Conflict

IT IS the nature of man to be in conflict with something. Some men are victorious; others are defeated. Those who are defeated as a rule leave few or no descendants. It follows that the psychology which is transmitted tends to be that of victors, and that where there is a fifty-fifty chance of victory, optimism will cause the chance to be overestimated. From the point of view of the survivors this is fortunate; the point of view of the vanquished is forgotten.

The contests in which men are engaged are of three kinds—they are conflicts of:

(1) Man and nature.
(2) Man and man.
(3) Man and himself.

These conflicts are very different in their character, and with the history of man their relative importance is continually changing. The methods by which the conflicts are conducted are completely different. Conflict with nature is conducted by physical science and technical skill. Conflict with man is conducted by politics and war. The inner conflict which rages in an individual soul has been dealt with hitherto by religion. There are now those who say that they can deal with it scientifically by the methods of psychoanalysis, but I doubt whether these methods unsupplemented can supply all that is needed.

Of these three kinds of contest, the contest with physical nature is in a sense the most fundamental, since victory in this contest is essential to survival. Men who perish in a glacial epoch or when hitherto fertile regions dry up or when earthquakes engulf whole valleys have lost their contest with physical nature; so have all those who die in famines and pestilences. Every victory over physical nature makes possible an increase in the numbers of the human species and has usually been used mainly to this end.

But in proportion as man masters his environment his relations to his fellow-men assume increasing importance, partly because the technique of mastery over nature involves social groups more coherent than those of the most primitive men, and partly because in proportion as the winning of daily bread becomes easier, a greater amount of energy can be set aside for the killing of enemies.

There comes, however, a moment in human evolution when, owing to the growth of technique, men can become richer through agreement with previous competitors than through extermination of enemies. When this stage is reached what may be called the demands of technique require a cessation, or at least mitigation, of the conflicts of man with man. When this stage is reached (it is, in fact, the stage which mankind has reached at the present moment) the conflicts that most need to be resolved are the conflicts of man with himself. The long ages of the other two kinds of conflict have molded human nature to a pattern formerly appropriate, but now technically obsolete. The ages of external warfare reflected themselves in an internal war in the soul. In this internal war in the soul, one part labeled the other "sin," and determined to vanquish it. But the victory was never so complete as in external conflicts, and after every defeat sin would again rear its ugly head.

This unending warfare within, which was originally a reflection of the warfare without, now became, on the contrary, a source of the warfare without. Sin is only part of my nature, but it is the whole nature of my enemies. So at least the old-fashioned moralist believes. And therefore the soul which is not at peace with itself cannot be at peace with the world, and external wars have to continue in order to hide from individual men that the real war is within. For these reasons the war of man with himself is that which at the end of human evolution assumes supreme importance.

Each kind of war should end in harmony. The conflict of man with physical nature is turned into a harmony in proportion as man learns the secrets of nature, and thereby becomes able to co-operate with her. The conflict of man with man serves a purpose so long as there is no possibility of adequate food-supply for all. But when the conquest of nature has secured the possibility of nourishment for everybody, and when the growth of technique has made large-scale co-operation profitable, the conflict of man with man becomes an anachronism, and should end in a political and economic unification such as is sought by the advocates of world government. By this means an external harmony of man with man can be established, but it will not be a stable harmony until men have achieved a genuine harmony within themselves, and have ceased to regard a part of themselves as an enemy to be vanquished. This, in a nutshell, is the history of man—past, present, and (I hope) future. In subsequent chapters I shall endeavor to fill in this bare outline.

Mastery over Physical Nature

M AN has had an existence which is long in relation to historical time, but short in relation to geological epochs. It is thought that he has existed for about a million years. There are those (for example, Einstein) who think that he has very likely run his course, and that within comparatively few years he will have succeeded in exterminating himself with superb scientific skill. For my part, I find it hard to take this extreme view, but if we are to avoid such a gloomy conclusion to the history of our species, it is as well that we should learn to take account of the demands of man as man, rather than of this or that group of men. For it is man as man that is now threatened by his own inability to think of the species as a whole. Man by the mastery of nature has emerged gradually into a degree of liberty for which he seems as yet insufficiently adult. I think that if he is to be persuaded to abstain from suicide, it is as well that he should remember the bright promise of his youth and gradual progress, which is now in danger of an abrupt end.

The early history of our remote ancestors is somewhat conjectural. They contained no Herodotus, anxious to give us information. What we know, we know from scanty remains, discovered by chance and interpreted by conjecture. What is to be said is therefore doubtful. But it is tedious to emphasize this doubt at every moment, and I shall therefore allow myself a certain degree of imaginative freedom in guessing at the life of our earliest human ancestors and their proximate progenitors.

Man, it would seem, has descended from arboreal apes. They lived a happy life in tropical forests, eating coconuts when they were hungry, and throwing them at each other when they were not. They were perpetually occupied in gymnastics, and acquired an agility which to us is truly astonishing. But after some millions of years of this arboreal paradise, their numbers increased to the point where the supply of coconuts was no longer adequate. The population problem set in, and was dealt with in two different ways: those who lived in the middle of the forest learned to throw coconuts with such accuracy as to disable adversaries, whose consequent death relieved the pressure of population, but those who lived on the edge of the forest found another method: they looked out over the fields and discovered that they yielded delicious fruits of various kinds quite as pleasant as coconuts, and gradually they came down from the trees and spent more and more time in the open on the ground. This had advantages and disadvantages: the obvious advantage was that it opened to them large territories previously inaccessible; the other advantage, which in the long run proved the more important one, was that since they did not need their arms and hands for climbing, they had the free use of them as tools. They soon discovered that if you live on the ground it is easy to pick up stones, which are more effective missiles than coconuts. They even came to know that stones with sharp edges are preferable to those that are more rounded. And so when later armies of arboreal apes tried to imitate their pioneering predecessors, they were met with volleys of sharp stones, to which they had no adequate reply, and the terrestrial apes won great victories by superiority in munitions. All this happened some ten million years ago, but I will not pretend to know the date exactly. For nine million years, or thereabouts, these terrestrial apes gradually extended their territory; whereas the arboreal apes had sought safety by superiority in gymnastics, the terrestrial apes scored most by intelligence. They discovered, for instance, that you could open an oyster shell with a stone, and the succulent result was the first prize for scholastic eminence. In the course of some nine million years, the brains of some of these apes gradually increased to the point which allows present-day anthropologists to classify them as human, or very nearly so.

Our first human ancestors were a very rare species. They lived under precarious conditions, exposed to the rigors of the weather, to the hostility of wild beasts, and to all the dangers of famine that could be caused by drought. They possessed no weapons, they probably had not mastered the use of fire, and if they had language of any sort it must have consisted of no more than a few cries. Their one weapon in the struggle for existence was intelligence, and intelligence at first was very far from being so powerful a weapon as it has become. The biological usefulness of intelligence consists largely in the possibility of transmitting experience. An animal may learn from another animal what it actually sees done, but it cannot learn through narrative; a man, when he has acquired language, can do so, and therefore the intelligence of each individual can become the property of the whole tribe, and each generation can hand on to the next a multitude of skills which would be beyond the power of any animal species to transmit. Animals do, it is true, educate their young up to a point; I have watched a father and mother sea-gull teach a young sea-gull how to dive, and the young sea-gull displayed just the same kind of shrinking timidity as a human child would have displayed. But it is only very simple things that animals can teach in this way, whereas men, by virtue of speech, can transmit anything that they know themselves. And so it happened that when our ancestors had reached a certain point in the development of intelligence, intelligence became, to generation after generation, an increasingly important factor of survival. It is true that for a long time it was inadequate for its purpose; many races of men died out; of the fossil men that anthropologists have discovered, only a small minority are thought to have been our ancestors. The rest were unsuccessful poor relations who gradually perished through ill luck or insufficient adaptability. But throughout the five hundred thousand years that came after the emergence of the first man, natural selection was at work, and the size of human brains gradually increased. About five hundred thousand years ago, nature seems (according to some authorities) to have decided that enough had been done in this way, and since then we have not grown any more intelligent. We learn more, it is true; we go to school; we go into workshops; we go into Government offices and study statistics. But it seems that (if these authorities are to be believed) the best men of five hundred thousand years ago, if they had been caught young and sent to school in a modern country, would have done just as well as modern children do. What they lacked was what is acquired, not what is congenital.

The life of these early men had advantages and disadvantages as compared with the life of civilized men in our own day. They were not over-crowded; they could roam for months without fear of meeting a stranger; physical necessity compelled them to take enough exercise, so that their livers were seldom out of order; they lived in small tribes of about a hundred individuals where everybody knew everybody, and where on the whole there was friendship within the tribe. Occasionally, no doubt, they would find themselves in conflict with another tribe, the vanquished would be exterminated, and the victors would annex their territory with the feeling that battle was great fun. But probably at first such battles were rare, because human beings were few.

The chief worry was as to food-supply. It is estimated that each individual at that time required at least two square miles for his subsistence, and even with two square miles at his disposal he would often be hungry, and not infrequently die for lack of nourishment.

Gradually, however, man emerged from these precarious conditions. Perhaps the first stage was the invention of primitive weapons, which enabled him to kill animals for food. Nobody knows at what stage men acquired the use of fire; perhaps it came late, perhaps early; whenever it did come it must have been a great boon. It enabled them to keep wild beasts at a distance; it enabled them to be warm at night, and at last, perhaps by accident, they discovered that it could be used for cooking.

The origin of language is also completely obscure. No doubt it began very gradually. Animals have a few cries that serve as signals, but even the highest apes, although anatomically they should be capable of speech, have not been found able to pronounce words, even with the most intensive professorial instruction. The superior brain of man is apparently a necessity for the mastering of speech. When man became sufficiently intelligent, we must suppose that he gradually increased the number of cries for different purposes. It was a great day when he discovered that speech could be used for narrative. There are those who think that in this respect picture language preceded oral language. A man could draw a picture on the wall of his cave to show in which direction he had gone, or what prey he hoped to catch. Probably picture language and oral language developed side by side. On the whole I am inclined to think that language has been the most important single factor in the development of man.

Two important stages came not so long before the dawn

of written history. The first was the domestication of animals; the second was agriculture. Agriculture, which began in the river valleys of Egypt and Mesopotamia, was a step in human progress to which subsequently there was nothing comparable until our own machine age. Agriculture made possible an immense increase in the numbers of the human species in the regions where it could be successfully practiced, but at first these regions were few. These were, in fact, only those in which nature fertilized the soil after each harvest. Agriculture met with violent resistance, analogous to that which our Ruskins and Samuel Butlers offered to machines. Pastoral nomads considered themselves vastly superior to the tame folk who stayed in one place and were enslaved to the soil. But although the nomads repeatedly won military victories, the physical comforts which the upper classes derived from agricultural serfs always prevailed in the end, and the area of agriculture gradually increased. Even now this process is not at an end, but what remains for it to achieve is no longer very important.

The only other fundamental technical advance that preceded the emergence of man into recorded history was the invention of writing. Writing, like spoken language, developed gradually. It developed out of pictures, but as soon as it had reached a certain stage, it made possible the keeping of records and the transmission of information to people who were not present when the information was given.

These successive inventions and discoveries—fire, speech, weapons, domestic animals, agriculture, and writing—made possible the existence of civilized communities. They supplied the whole fundamental apparatus upon which civilized man subsisted for a very long time. From about 3000 B.C. until less than two hundred years ago there was no technical advance comparable to these. During this long period man had time to become accustomed to his technique, and to develop the beliefs and political organizations appropriate to it. There was, of course, an immense extension in the area of civilized life. At first it had been confined to the Nile, the Euphrates, the Tigris, and the Indus, but at the end of the period in question it covered much the greater part of the habitable globe. I do not mean to suggest that there was no technical progress during this long time; there was progress—there were even two inventions of very great importance, namely gunpowder and the mariner's compass—but neither of these can be compared in their revolutionary power to such things as speech and writing and agriculture.

Towards the end of the eighteenth century, man entered upon a new phase, involving a change as fundamental as that involved in the adoption of agriculture; I mean, of course, machine production and the application of science to industry. Physical science, one may say, has existed as a powerful element in culture for about 350 years. Machine production has existed for about half that time. During the period since its invention it has shown itself to be a revolutionary force of quite amazing intensity. As yet this has been almost solely operative in man's relation to nature, but by revolutionizing man's relation to nature, it has destroyed the old equilibrium that existed in man's relation to other men and to himself. The revolutions that it demands in these two provinces are still to seek, and it is the fact that they are still to seek which is the main cause of the present troubles of the world.

The specially human activities which distinguish man from other animals all depend upon the lessening of his bondage to physical nature. So long as he had to spend all his time in food-gathering, he could not devote much of his energy to war or politics or theology or science. These things are off-shoots of the productivity of labor; they depend upon the excess of one man's production over one man's consumption of food. The greater this excess becomes, the more possible it becomes for a man to devote himself to politics and war and culture and such luxuries.

Increase in agricultural productivity can be used in two ways: it can be used to increase the share of each, or it can be used to increase the number of those who share. In general, except in Western countries in quite recent years, increase in the productivity of labor has been devoted mainly to increase of numbers. If, like the behaviorists, we were to judge man's desires by what he does, we should infer that the thing he desires most ardently is an increase of the population of the world. In early times, as we saw, one person to every two square miles was as much as the land would support, and that only where it had considerable natural fertility. England at the present day supports a population of about 750 per square mile, that is to say, fifteen hundred times as many as it could support before human skills had been invented. This, of course, depends mainly upon industry, not upon agriculture, but if we take India and Pakistan, which are mainly agricultural, we find a population of 274 per square mile. These, as we know, are for the most part very near the lowest level at which life can be supported; that is to say, the inhabitants of India and Pakistan have chosen to employ the techniques of civilization almost entirely for the purpose of increase of population, to the exclusion of increase of happiness and culture. Although this has been the general rule throughout the world until quite recent times, there has been some slight overflow into other kinds of progress. It has been possible, in the period before machine production developed, to set apart a certain portion of the population for other purposes than for the production of food. There have been aristocracies and priests; there have been armies and navies; there have even been philosophers and artists, though they were too few to appear in statistical tables. Pharaoh and Nebuchadnezzar, Socrates and Plato, Buddha and

Mohammed, Leonardo and Bach, all were only possible because the food producers could produce more than they could eat. But when one considers such a community as the United States in the present day one finds a new phenomenon, namely that the great majority of the population enjoy very many things over and above the bare necessaries of life, and yet, in spite of this, very large parts of the population are not engaged in production, whether agricultural or industrial. There are all the young people who are still being educated after they have become able-bodied. There are the armed forces. There are the journalists and all the people concerned in the production of reading matter. There are teachers, clergy, politicans, and functionaries. All these people, from the point of view of primitive man, are luxuries, but a modern community would be impossible without at least some of them.

The liberation from bondage to nature has left men, in theory, free to choose their own ends to a degree that was never possible at any earlier time. I say "in theory," because impulses incorporated into human nature by long ages of training and natural selection remain to determine human action independently of present physical needs. What a nation can spare from increasing its own numbers, it devotes only in part to its own welfare. To a very great extent it devotes its energies to killing other people or preparing to kill them, or paying those who have helped to kill them in the past. In the United States about one-fifth of the total production of the country is being spent in rearmament. The freedom from bondage to nature, therefore, is by no means wholly a boon. It is only a boon in so far as the resulting liberty of choice leads to an increase of those activities which are of use to mankind as a whole. But in so far as it merely liberates combative impulses it does no good at all but quite the opposite. Some people tell fine stories of the use of atomic energy in industry, and the economies which will result. Such economies, if the world remains politically what it is now, will do nothing but harm, since they will set free a greater part of human energy for the purpose of mutual destruction. This example illustrates the way in which our new mastery of nature brings new responsibilities and new duties. If men prove incapable of this adaptation, the whole movement of science and scientific technique will have proved a misfortune, and perhaps will have taken man along a blind alley. While we were slaves to nature we could allow ourselves a slave mentality, and leave to nature decisions which now must be ours. This is difficult, since great parts of traditional religion and morality were inspired by man's bondage to nature, and the ways of thought and feeling that we acquire from our culture and from our early upbringing are hard to overcome, even when circumstances imperatively demand a different outlook. I am not pretending that man is omnipotent; on the contrary, I shall be concerned in the next chapter with the limits of human power. But I am concerned to say that these limits are much less narrow for modern scientific man than they were for our ancestors, and that no precise boundary can be set beyond which the limits cannot be made to recede. Innumerable facts of nature which once were inexorable data are now opportunities. Deserts are a challenge; Australian rivers can be made to flow from east to west instead of from west to east; before long it will be possible to demolish inconvenient parts of mountain ranges, and I dare say that by means of radioactivity the Polar ice will be melted. It will not be long before it becomes possible to travel to the moon. We already know how to combat many kinds of pestilence, and we may hope to eliminate other kinds before long. Our nomad ancestors, while they watched their flocks by night, observed the stars in their inexorable courses, and believed themselves subject to the influences of celestial bodies. Wind and storm, drought and heat, comets and meteors and plagues filled their lives with awe, and they hoped to escape by means of humility. Modern man does not combat plagues by humility; he has found that they are to be combated by scientific knowledge. Scientific knowledge, in fact, gives the means (when there are means) of combating any extra-human enemy, but it does not give the means of combating the human enemy without, or the part of the individual soul which leads it towards death rather than towards life. The problems of man's contest with nature, in so far as they are soluble, can be solved by physical science, but they are not the only problems with which man is faced. For his other problems, other methods are necessary.

The Limits of Human Power

THE old humility of the shepherds who felt themselves subject to the influences of Pleiades is no longer appropriate in the scientific world. But there is a danger lest it should be replaced by a species of arrogance towards nature, which can lead to great disasters. Man, however scientific he may be, is not omnipotent. He is hedged in by natural limits. By means of his knowledge and technique he can diminish the narrowness of these limits, but he can never remove them wholly. Some astronomers try to cheer us up in moments of depression by assuring us that one fine day the sun will explode, and in the twinkling of an eye we shall all be turned into gas. I do not know whether this is going to happen, nor when it will happen if it does happen, but I think it is safe to say that if it does it will be a matter outside human control, and that even the best astronomers will be unable to prevent it. This is an extreme example, and one which it is useless to think about, because there is no way in which human behavior can be adapted to it. It does, however, serve one purpose, which is to remind us that we are not gods. You may exclaim indignantly, "but I never thought we were!" No doubt, dear reader, you are not one of those who suffer from the most extreme follies of our age, for if you were, you would not be one of my readers. But if you consider the Politbureau or the American technocrats you will see that there are those who escape atheism by impiously imagining themselves on the throne of the Almighty. Such men have forgotten that while we can coax physical nature into satisfying many of our wishes, we cannot exercise authority over it or make it change its ways one jot. The Russian Government appears to think that Soviet decrees can change the laws of genetics; the Vatican apparently believes that ecclesiastical decrees could secure adequate nourishment for us all, even if there were only standing room on the planet. Such opinions, to my mind, represent a form of insane megolomania entirely alien to the scientific spirit.

There are two very different elements in science: scientific knowledge and scientific technique. Those whom I am calling technocrats are interested solely in scientific technique, and the more extreme among them deny that there is such a thing as scientific knowledge, or indeed any kind of knowledge. Scientific theorists, on the other hand, are concerned to discover natural laws, and leave to others the discovery of practical ways in which such laws can be useful. In a word, the technocrat wishes to change nature, while the theorist wishes to understand it. There is practically no one left in the world who will maintain that the point of view of the theorist alone is adequate, but there are many who think that the point of of view of the technocrat suffices. Or if at moments they feel it somewhat arid they supplement it, not by any doubt that can be entertained by a scientific inquirer, but by an unscientific form of arrogance, namely the belief that, without the patience and without the submission involved in observing nature, we can arrive by a form of self-assertion at kinds of knowledge which science is incapable of supplying. This again is megolomania. Man is neither impotent nor omnipotent, he has powers and his powers are surprisingly great, but they are not infinite and they are not so great as he might wish.

But let us have done with these generalities. It is not the generalities but their practical application with which I am concerned. How long will it be before the accessible oil in the world is exhausted? Will all the arable land be turned into dust-bowls as it has been in large parts of the United States? Will the population increase to the point where men again, like their remote ancestors, have no leisure to think of anything but the food supply? Such questions are not to be decided by general philosophical reflections. Communists think that there will be plenty of oil if there are no capitalists. Some religious people think that there will be plenty of food if we trust in Providence. Such ideas are superficial, even when they are called scientific, as they are by the Communists.

Modern industry depends upon raw materials which are found at, or near, the earth's surface. These raw materials are the product of past geological ages; for the most part they are not being reproduced by any natural process. The elements were built up long ago by a process which we are just beginning to understand, and which when understood may enable clever men to put an end to the human race. The process by which the elements were built up required enormous heat, the sort of heat that exists in the interior of the sun. In a great natural laboratory, nature, starting with hydrogen, arrived by various stages at a number of elements. The number used to be ninety-two but is now indefinite. The elements, at temperatures much lower than that at which they were formed, entered into chemical combinations. At a certain stage the earth was at a temperature peculiarly suitable to the formation of complex chemical combinations, and at last combinations were formed which had the properties that are characteristic of living matter. Living matter has a curious property which I have called "chemical imperialism." In virtue of this property, when it is put into a suitable environment, it transforms a mass of dead matter into a mass of living matter. It is this property which has made organic evolution possible.

The processes we have been studying are processes of synthesis. They proceed from the simpler to the more complex. The processes of modern industry do exactly the reverse. They use complex raw material and simplify it. So far, this process of simplification is, in the main, not reversible by scientific methods. It may be that it will become so. There is already a hope of turning hydrogen atoms into helium atoms; this is the process which, when perfected, will give us the blessings of the hydrogen bomb. But in all such processes, so far as science is able to control them, there is waste. What is built up in one place is built up by means of dissolution in another place. If by enormous heat we turn a little hydrogen into helium, we shall have turned a very much larger amount of matter into diffused heat which will never again be usable. Many of the processes of nature are irreversible, and these processes are essential in any form of scientific industry that can at present be imagined. In the reign of Edward III, coal lay about on the surface of the ground. People picked it up and used it at home. The smoke was found to be such a nuisance that the burning of coal was made illegal. I do not know whether this law has ever been repealed, or whether, like the law against polytheism, it has been merely forgotten. However that may be, the obtaining of coal is not now the easy process that it was in the fourteenth century, and there is every reason to suppose that more and more human labor will be required to supply a given amount of coal. Many ages ago, the energy supplied by the sun's heat was transformed into luxuriant vegetation. The energy lay locked up in the layers of petrified tropical ferns until ruthless industrialists seized it and transformed it back again into heat. But the heat that we generate when we burn coal is not localized like the heat in the sun, and is not continually regenerated by atomic processes. It floats off into the atmosphere and becomes forever useless. There is no process in nature, and there is none imaginable to human ingenuity, by which heat, once diffused, can be reconcentrated, or by which when diffused it can serve any human purpose.

All sources of energy upon which industry depends are wasted when they are employed; and industry is expending them at a continually increasing rate. Already coal has been largely replaced by oil, and oil is being used up so fast that East and West alike conceive it necessary to their own prosperity to destroy the industry of the other. And what is true of oil is equally true of other natural resources. Every day, many square miles of forest are turned into newspaper, but there is no known process by which newspaper can be turned into forest. You will say that this need not worry us, since newspapers will be replaced by radio, but radio requires electricity, electricity requires power, and power depends upon raw materials.

Modern industry, in fact, is a kind of rape. All the long astronomical and geological ages during which the materials which we find useful have been built up, contribute a moment's blaze, a moment's frivolous exuberance. But when his fireworks are finished, what will become of industrial man?

All this, of course, does not appear in practice in the tragic and catastrophic form in which I have been stating it. What we know is that the price of coal goes up, and we do not readily connect this fact with the second law of thermodynamics. If you look up this law in a textbook, you will learn that it states that entropy always increases, and if you are not a physicist you will not be much the wiser. But the law can be stated more simply, and is stated more simply by proverbial wisdom. It states, in fact, that you cannot unscramble eggs. It deals with all the irreversible processes of nature. Some processes are reversible, some are not. If you travel from

London to Edinburgh, you can also travel from Edinburgh to London, but if coal is used to make your train go, there is no way by which you can collect the heat which it generates, and turn it back into coal. If you shuffle a pack of cards, you can, if you take enough trouble, unshuffle them again, but if you drop a drop of ink into a glass of water, the ink will gradually spread throughout the water, and there is no way by which you can collect it back again into a drop. All industry depends upon such irreversible processes; it all uses up the earth's capital. Modern industry is, in fact, a spendthrift, and sooner or later must suffer the penalty of spendthrifts.

I know that most people meet such considerations with a kind of facile optimism; they say "Oh, the men of science are sure to think of some clever invention, and even if they don't it will last my time." They feel like the proverbial Irishman—"Why should I do anything for posterity; it never did anything for me!" But I am concerned in this book with Man, considered as a single creature with a single biography. I cannot be content with a brief moment of riotous living followed by destitution, and however clever the scientists may be, there are some things that they cannot be expected to achieve. When they have used up all the easily available sources of energy that nature has scattered carelessly over the surface of our planet, they will have to resort to more laborious processes, and these will involve a gradual lowering of the standard of living. Modern industrialists are like men who have come for the first time upon fertile virgin land, and can live for a little while in great comfort with only a modicum of labor. It would be irrational to hope that the present heyday of industrialism will not develop far beyond its present level, but sooner or later, owing to the exhaustion of raw material, its capacity to supply human needs will diminish, not suddenly, but gradually. This could, of course, be prevented if men exercised any restraint or foresight in their present frenzied exploitation. Perhaps before it is too late they will learn to do so. But this is a question of politics, and I do not wish, as yet, to consider the political aspect of our problem.

So far I have been considering the raw materials of industry, but the matter is far more grave as regards soil, which is the raw material of food. Ever since agriculture began it has been carried on wastefully in most parts of the world. Where methods are completely primitive, the cultivator merely moves on after he has exhausted the soil of one piece of land. This requires, of course, a great deal of available territory, and even then, only offers a permanent solution if the damage done to the soil by cultivation is temporary and not permanent. It is no wonder that men worshiped fertility divinities or that they developed a belief in the magical efficacy of human sacrifice. But in former times, while the population of the globe was still sparse, the problem had not the tragic importance that it has in our own day. It has been treated very fully in two books: Fairfield Osborne's *Our Plundered Planet* and William Vogt's *Road to Survival*. I could wish to see both these books carefully studied by all who allow themselves a facile optimism, and especially by those who believe that free enterprise and the profit motive will solve all problems. They will learn from these authors many tragic facts about formerly fertile hillsides now turned into barren rock, about irrigated plains now desert, and flourishing civilizations now buried beneath the sands. They will learn that this process, which devastated Western Asia and North Africa centuries ago, is in full swing at the present day in many parts of the Western hemisphere, including the United States. They will learn that the intense demand for food, which results from increase of population and development of industry, is becoming year by year more difficult to satisfy. We all know that the price of food goes up, but most of us attribute this to the wickedness of the Government. If we live under a progressive Government, it makes us reactionary; if we live under a reactionary Government, it turns us into Socialists. Both these reactions are superficial and frivolous. All Governments, whatever their political complexion, are at present willy-nilly in the grip of natural forces which can only be dealt with by a degree of intelligence of which mankind hitherto has shown little evidence.

I have been speaking hitherto in this chapter of what can be expected on the basis of our present scientific knowledge. It must be admitted, however, that there are favorable possibilities which would bring about, at least for a time, a quite different state of affairs. There are those who tell us that the use of soil for growing plants is quite out of date, and that they can be grown just as well without, by supplying proper chemicals in proper proportions. I have a doubt whether they would taste quite as nice by this process, but I suppose a small quantity of food could still be grown by the old methods for the benefit of captains of industry and the Politbureau. As for the rest of the population, they will have to learn to be scientific in their tastes, and be content with whatever in the way of calories and vitamins the experts consider good for them.

Apart from the question of food, there is the question of energy. It seems clear that, if it were financially worth while, fairly economical methods could be discovered by which more use would be made than at present of energy from the sun. And in theory there is no calculable limit to what can be got out of atomic energy. When people have discovered how to turn hydrogen into helium, sea-water will become their raw material, and it will be a long time before this source of supply is exhausted. Speaking of less specific possibilities, we have to reflect that man has existed for about a million years, and scientific technique for at most two hundred years. Seeing what it has already accomplished, it would be very rash to place any limits upon what it may accomplish in the future.

Scientific knowledge is an intoxicating draught, and it may be one which the human race is unable to sustain. It may be that, like the men who built the Tower of Babel in the hope of reaching up to heaven, so the men who pursue the secrets of the atom will be punished for their impiety by providing by accident the means of exterminating the human species, and perhaps all life on this planet. From some points of view such a consummation might not be wholly regrettable, but these points of view can hardly be ours. Perhaps somewhere else, in some distant nebula, some unimportant star has an unimportant planet on which there are rational beings. Perhaps in another million years their instruments will tell them of our fate, and lead them to agree on an agenda for a conference of foreign ministers. If so, man will not have lived in vain.

V

Population

THERE are many points of view from which the life of man may be considered. There are those who think of him primarily in cultural terms as a being capable of lofty art and sublime speculation and discovery of the hidden secrets of nature. There are those who think of him as one of those kinds of animal that are capable of government, though in this respect he is completely outshone by ants and bees. There are those who think of him as the master of war; these include all the men in all countries who decide upon the adornment of public squares, where it is an invariable rule obeyed by all right-thinking public authorities that the most delectable object to be seen by the passers-by is a man on horseback, who is commemorated for his skill in homicide. But apart from all these views of man, in which we celebrate matters in which he is distinguished from many other species of animals, he may be viewed also as just one among animal species, concerned like the others in competition or co-operation with other species, and other members of his own species. When we consider a species biologically, we consider it as if it had a desire to increase its numbers to the uttermost. I do not mean that we really attribute such a desire to it; nobody supposes, for example, that oysters are impressed with the importance of the multiplication of their species. But although no species of animals has this desire, most species of animals behave as they would if they had it. This applies also to most human beings at most times. Most human beings at most times have behaved as if they thought that the most important thing that they could do would be to leave a multitude of descendants.

As everyone knows, Malthus pointed out that the single-hearted pursuit of this aim was likely to have certain unpleasant consequences. The unpleasant consequences that he foresaw depended upon the law of diminishing returns. The law of diminishing returns states that after a certain amount of labor and capital has been applied to a piece of land, an increase in the labor and capital applied will not yield a proportionate return. That is to say, supposing from an acre of land, by means of a given amount of labor and capital, you raise a certain number of bushels of wheat, and supposing you then double the amount of labor and capital that you apply to that acre, you will not get twice as many bushels of wheat as you got before. It follows that, if you possess just enough land to provide a comfortable sustenance for yourself and your wife, you may not have enough to provide a comfortable sustenance for yourself and your wife and two able-bodied sons, still less for yourself and your wife and ten able-bodied sons. It follows further (I am still taking the argument in a completely abstract form and ignoring all necessary limitations) that any increase in population in a given area beyond a certain point entails increase of poverty, and ultimately reaches a maximum beyond which further increase is rendered impossible by starvation. Malthus, in his comfortable parsonage, applied this doctrine to the laboring poor, and was thereby relieved of any necessity to try to ameliorate their sorrows, which he had proved to his satisfaction to be arithmetically inevitable. Darwin, as everybody also knows, ex-

tended the doctrine of Malthus to the whole animal and vege-
table kingdoms, and thus gave cosmic importance to the economics of the Manchester school. The economics of the
Manchester school are now out of date, and this makes people
suppose that Malthus's doctrines must be mistaken. There is no
doubt that they were in part mistaken, but I think we must
also admit that they were in part true. It is important to dis-
entangle the true and false parts in the teaching of Malthus.

To begin with the law of diminishing returns: where agriculture is concerned, this becomes true at a certain point. If
you turn a single man loose on virgin soil, he cannot produce
as much as he would if he had helpers. How many helpers he
needs before he reaches a maximum production per head depends upon technique. A primitive food-gatherer probably
gains nothing by co-operation, or, at any rate, very little,
whereas a modern agriculturalist, whose farm is industrialized,
requires a multitude of helpers before he reaches a maximum
of efficiency. He needs expensive machinery, which is only
profitable when it is employed over a large area, and in support of a number of men. He needs a railway to carry away
his produce. He needs a telephone. He needs fertilizers, which
may be brought from a considerable distance, and he probably
needs foreign markets. The consequence of all this is that a
very considerable population is required to reach the maximum of production per head, and until this is reached, production obeys a law of increasing returns. In the Old Testament, a large family is considered a blessing, and it was so in
the circumstances in which the Patriarchs lived. The Mor-
mons, who lived in similar circumstances, took a similar view
about increase of population. But in any given state of technique, there is in agriculture an optimum for the application
of labor and capital to a given area of land. This optimum
yields the greatest return to labor and capital; when the
amount of labor or capital is either increased or diminished,

the return per unit is less. It follows that, in any given state of technique, increase of population beyond a certain point involves a lowering in the standard of life. Whether this lowering will be universal or will be confined to laborers and their families depends upon the social system. But it is inevitable that when increase of population goes beyond a certain point, the lowering in the standard of life should apply to the large majority of the population.

Two things follow: one, that in any given state of technique, increase of population in a sparsely populated area may bring increase of prosperity; the other, that the development of scientific technique tends to increase the optimum density of population. The most obvious instance of this is the United States. It is not by any means clear that the wealth per head of the inhabitants of the United States would be greater if the population were less, but that depends upon the existence of an extremely elaborate technique. The population of Red Indians in the days before white settlement could not have been greatly increased without destroying the sources of supply upon which that population depended, and so bringing about disastrous destitution.

But although the Malthusian limit can always be pushed back by improving technique, there are always limits beyond which it cannot be pushed. To take an extreme hypothesis: it would obviously be impossible for mankind to have an adequate supply of food if there were only just standing room for the human race. And without imagining so extreme an hypothesis, there is, in any given society at any given time, a very considerable possibility that increase of population may outstrip improvement in technique, and therefore cause a general lowering in the standard of life.

This, in fact, is happening at the present time throughout very large parts of the world. There seems to be little doubt that the inhabitants of the Indus valley were more prosperous and generally happier three thousand years ago than they are now. In India generally there has been an increase of poverty among the peasants in recent times. And what is true of India is true of Southeast Asia generally, of most parts of Africa, and of the tropical parts of Latin America. In most of these regions, modern medicine has brought about a fall in the death-rate, but not in the birth-rate. It has thereby contributed to human misery.

Early man could only live in warm climates, and, as mentioned before, each individual required about two square miles to supply him with food. However, various stages marked his advances in the problem of getting food. First came simple weapons which enabled him to hunt. Then came domestication of useful animals. Then came agriculture. Last (so far) came the industrial revolution.

It is supposed that agriculture began about 8000 B.C., and Julian Huxley [1] estimates that just before it began the human population of the globe was about ten million. He adds the following estimates:

5000 B.C.	..	..	..	..	20 million.
A.D. 400	..	..	..	..	200 million.
A.D. 1650	..	..	..	..	540 million.
A.D. 1950	..	..	..	..	2,200 million.

The present rate of increase in the world's population (which has continued steadily throughout the two world wars) is about 1.16 per cent per annum. Every day there are 70,000 more people in the world than there were the day before; every year there are 25 million more. At the present rate, in a hundred years there will be 5,400 million; in two hundred, 14,500 million; in three hundred, 45,000 million.

There are two ways of checking increase of population: one is by increasing the death-rate, the other by diminishing the birth-rate. Old-fashioned moralists tell us that the first is virtu-

[1] "Population and Human Destiny," *World Review*, January 1950. The following estimates are quoted from this article.

ous, the second wicked. True, the first involves vast and terrible suffering, while the second involves no suffering at all. But what of that? We ought to think of the next world, not of this one. Those who believe that a benevolent Creator insists upon either misery in this life or eternal torment in the next are welcome to their opinion, but I do not think it is one which ought to control practical statesmanship. Malthus held that there were only three restraints to the growth of population: moral restraint, vice, and misery. He had little hope of moral restraint, and as a clergyman he condemned vice; he therefore advocated misery—of course, only for the lower orders. I hope the world has advanced beyond this point of view during the 150 years since Malthus wrote. I hope those who control the world's policy are now ready to admit that what is necessary in order to preserve mankind from wretchedness is not to be labeled "vice."

So long as we consider mankind as a whole, as a biological species engaged in adjusting itself to its environment, it is obvious what ought to be done to cope with the population problem. There ought to be universal instruction in birth-control, with penalties for those who have too many children. By these means Governments could, if they chose, easily arrest the increase of population within a generation.

But unfortunately mankind are divided into nations, and the apparent interests of individual nations are by no means always in harmony with the interests of mankind. We must therefore now consider the population problem, not in the world as a whole, but in various different regions and nations, not forgetting its sinister connection with power politics.

From the point of view of population statistics, the world at present is divided into two rather sharply contrasted groups. There are nations where birth-rate and death-rate are both low, and others where both are high. Those with low rates are: Western Europe, North America, and the white population of the British Dominions. Those with high rates are: U.S.S.R., Asia, Africa (except whites), Central and South America.

In the century and a half from 1750 to 1900 the population of Europe and North America increased from 141 million to 482 million. This increase has now nearly ceased, and probably will soon cease completely, except in Eastern Europe. In fact, the white population of the world (excluding the U.S.S.R. and its dependencies) may be expected soon to become stationary.

In other parts of the world we find a very different state of affairs. There is no evidence of a fall in the birth-rate, but, wherever white men are in control, there has been a very rapid fall in the death-rate. Population outside what I am calling the Western area is therefore increasing quite as fast as it did in England in the nineteenth century.

I will begin with a very remarkable set of figures for Japan, given in the London *Times* of March 8, 1950. This shows the effect of American administration.

The population of Japan had doubled in the sixty years preceding 1945. During the second world war, in spite of atom-bombs and the incendiary bombing of the large cities, the population increased by about 5 million; in the three years from 1946 to 1949 it increased by about 6 million. The death-rate in 1946 was 15.58; in 1948, 11.96. This is an extraordinarily rapid fall for so short a period as two years. The causes of this decline may be indicated by a single fact: in 1946 there were 17,800 cases of smallpox; in 1948 there were 29 cases.

The population of Japan is now 82 million, and the excess of births over deaths is 1,600,000 a year.

The area of Japan is not large, and in present circumstances every increase of population means increase of poverty. Both American and Japanese authorities are profoundly disquieted by this situation.

India (including Pakistan) has a very rapidly increasing

population, with high birth- and death-rates, but the latter has diminished more than the former. The increase of population in ten years in India exceeds the whole population of Great Britain. The population is about 400 million and has been increasing by about 15 per cent every ten years. The death-rate fell from 35.9 in 1922 to 22.2 in 1939. The birth-rate in 1939 was 33.6, as compared with 15.3 in England.

The population problem in India is generally acknowledged to be acute. To quote the *Manchester Guardian* of April 26, 1951:

The Government of India has published the provisional figures of its recent census. The population (exclusive of Jammu and Kashmir) numbers 357 million. In spite of the mortality from the great Bengal famine, it has increased by 13.4 per cent since 1941. In the last twenty years the rate of growth has been three times what it was at the beginning of the century. Every year India's need for food increases by half a million tons of grain. For the whole country, the density of population is three hundred to the square mile; this is six times as great as in the United States. The ever-increasing pressure on the soil in India is the main problem of South Asia. It is forcing the country towards a poverty which will probably end in revolution; it is one of the main causes of the famine now threatening. A memorandum of these facts should be constantly on the table of everybody concerned with Asian affairs; that and Malthus's essay. Even if the Colombo Plan were carried out, production would still be running a losing race with population. Mr. Nehru says that the Government of India is now studying the possibilities of birth-control. The difficulties in a country with an illiterate and impoverished people are great. But what else can save India? Prosperity and education together might eventually cause, in India, as elsewhere, a falling birth-rate. But the death-rate also would fall. Until there is some decline in the number of new mouths, devouring every increase in the national income, prosperity will be a mocking and empty concept.

Every rational person must be glad to find that Mr. Nehru recognizes the need of birth-control in India. On this subject the international edition of the New York *Times* for April 20, 1951, reports:

POPULATION 43

Birth-control and other methods of curbing India's rapidly growing population are being studied by the Government, Prime Minister Jawaharlal Nehru said today in an interview.

Mr. Nehru said he favored birth-control as a long-range project
for cutting the 4,000,000-a-year increase in this country's population and as one of the measures needed to solve the food crisis.

While the Hindu and Moslem religions that predominate in this
subcontinent do not prohibit the practice of birth-control, many
of the nation's 362,000,000 people oppose it through superstition or
belief that it is against the laws of nature.

Mr. Nehru said India was overpopulated by American standards
but was not by European standards and, being a big country,
"should support a big population."

India's population averages about 300 persons to the square mile,
six times the average in the United States. Europeans are often even
more crowded. The average is 750 to the square mile in Belgium,
530 in Britain and almost 400 in Italy.

India, like the United States, contains its quota of cruel
bigots, who prefer poverty, famine, and war to birth-control.
One must hope that Pandit Nehru's influence will be sufficient
to combat such sinister superstition.

The U.S.S.R. has a population of about 200 million, which
is estimated to be increasing rapidly.

Russia, India, China, and Japan contain between them about
half the population of the globe. If there is no change in vital
statistics, they will soon contain much more than half. On the
other hand, the population of what we may call the "Western"
group, even liberally interpreted, is less than a quarter of the
total population of the world, and is likely soon to be much less
than a quarter.

I pass now to another part of the world, namely, Africa.
Here I will take as typical of the Negro portions the Colony of
Kenya. The Kenya branch of the British Medical Association
in December 1947 presented a Memorandum to the Home
Government on Health and Population in His Majesty's Dependencies in Africa. I rely upon this Memorandum in what
follows.

During the 25 years preceding 1947 there was a 50 per cent loss of soil fertility. Meanwhile the population was increasing at the rate of 1.5 per cent per annum, rising up to nearly 2 per cent. As might be expected in these circumstances, grinding poverty is increasing. Unless drastic steps are taken, within twenty years large importations of food will be necessary to prevent major recurrent famines. Even if everything possible is done to increase productivity, there is no hope, according to these medical authorities, except in birth-control. Otherwise the standard of life, already appallingly low, is bound to fall still further.

The conditions are substantially the same throughout Negro Africa.

There is a close correlation between vital statistics and standards of life. On the one hand there are nations which have a low birth-rate, a low death-rate, and a nearly stationary population; these countries have a standard of life which is high and improving. On the other hand there are nations with a high birth-rate, a high death-rate, and a rapidly increasing population; these countries have a standard of life which is low and deteriorating. Moreover, the poor and prolific nations are at least twice as numerous as the rich and unprolific nations.

This situation is menacing, not only to the richer nations, but to mankind. Paradoxically, the menace is greatest where white men govern non-white populations, as in Africa, formerly in India, and now in Japan. In such countries, white men, by medical science, diminish the death-rate but not the birth-rate; they thus accelerate the plunge towards misery and the attendant revolutionary fury. So long as religious prejudice prevents white men from teaching birth-control, they inevitably must, however humane their intentions, increase the sum of misery and degradation in non-white territories that they govern.

The importance of the population problem, although it is

obvious to all who are concerned in the administration of
countries with a high birth-rate, is minimized in almost all
official publications for fear of offending those who think it
wicked to do what is necessary for the alleviation of human
misery. It is to be hoped that the men who at present hold
these views will gradually modify them, as many other cruel
doctrines formerly held by theologians have been modified.
It is difficult for kindly men to continue indefinitely to believe
anything that involves vast unhappiness, whether in this life or
in the next, and I hope that those who, as yet, persist in doctrines having this effect will cease to hold them when the
results to mankind become obvious to them. I should like, in
this respect, to quote a letter from Professor Julian Huxley in
The Times of March 13, 1951. He says:

I was glad to see Mr. Brander, in your issue of March 7, stressing
the need for a world population policy. When I was Director-
General of Unesco I urged the Economic and Social Council of the
United Nations to follow up the valuable conference on world
resources which, with the collaboration of the World Health Organization, Unesco, the Food and Agriculture Organization, and
other specialized agencies, it held in 1948 by organizing a comparable conference on the population which consumes the resources.
This would at least bring the problem officially on to the international stage, and I still hope that such a conference will take place
in the not too distant future.

Meanwhile the problem becomes steadily more acute. The daily
net addition to the world's population is now nearly 60,000, as
against about half that when I was born, and is steadily rising. Even
more alarming is the fact that the rate of increase of world population (compound interest rate a year) is also steadily increasing, in
spite of the falling off in regions like Western Europe.

In the last couple of months there have been references in your
columns to difficulties caused by over-population in Kenya, Japan,
British Honduras, Italy, Puerto Rico, parts of North Africa, Cyprus,
Uganda, the British West Indies, the South African Protectorates,
Egypt and Haiti; and even where over-population is not yet evident
there may be an alarmingly rapid rate of increase, as in Formosa,
many parts of Latin America, French Canada, parts of West and
Central Africa, etc.

From all such detailed instances two general points stand out: First, that the mere quantitative increase in numbers is creating a qualitatively new situation for the human species; and, secondly, as Mr. Brander rightly stressed, that all ameliorative measures aimed at increasing production are merely palliatives and, in the perspective of history, extremely short-term ones: in two or three generations they will be overtaken by human multiplication and the world will be where it was before, only a little worse off, since some of its vacant spaces and unused resources will have been taken up.

It is imperative that we should develop a rational population policy for the world as a whole and should work out methods for putting it into practice (including methods for overcoming current objections and prejudices on the matter). The first step towards this, I still consider, should be taken by the United Nations.

There would be little difficulty in causing the practice of birth-control to spread throughout the regions which at present are most threatened by increase of population. All that is needed is to spread the knowledge required, and self-interest can be relied upon to do the rest. Certainly a considerable spread of education is involved, but that is in any case desirable. There are some who think that industrialization alone will lead to a fall in the birth-rate, but I do not think the facts bear this out. When England became industrialized, the birth-rate at first did not fall, and the increase of population became much more rapid than before. It was the prosecution of Bradlaugh and Mrs. Besant for birth-control propaganda in the year 1878 that inaugurated the fall in the birth-rate. In France, which was mainly agricultural, the fall had begun sooner. I do not think that the desirable fall in the birth-rate would have come about except by an increase of education, accompanied by opportunities for ascertaining methods of birth-control.

It is a curious fact that those who are led to advocate birth-control through a study of Malthus's doctrines, although they are sometimes called neo-Malthusians, are really reverting to a doctrine which preceded Malthus, and suggested his doctrines to him. The principle of population was really discovered not by Malthus but by Condorcet, who, however, avoided the pessimistic conclusions which gave Malthus so much pleasure, by supplementing the doctrine with the advocacy of birth-control. Malthus, as a clergyman, thought birth-control wicked, and as a Manchester economist, enjoyed the iron law of wages, which assumed that wage-earners, though poor, would remain prolific. It is a pity that it was these doctrines, and not those of Condorcet, which acquired wide publicity.

The adoption of birth-control by large prosperous nations has shown a new possibility of general prosperity throughout the world. Natural impulses have led animals and men to breed faster than nature can support them, with the result that many had to die prematurely, and those who became adult very frequently perished from hunger. This was the mechanism of evolution—a mechanism involving vast suffering throughout the animal kingdom. The same mechanism persists to the present day in many parts of the world, China, India, Africa, tropical America among others. Those who urge that by means of technical advances a continually growing population can remain prosperous for an indefinite period are evidently incapable of appreciating the properties of geometrical progression. If population continues to increase, however slowly, it must ultimately surpass any assigned limit. Naturally this is impossible, since there is a limit to what the earth can yield; and as the population increases beyond a point, the earth must yield less, since a large amount of the earth's surface must be withdrawn from agriculture. But if population is not to increase without limit, one of two things must happen: either the birth-rate must be low, or the death-rate must be high. Those who oppose birth-control, if they are capable of a little arithmetic, will have to admit that their opposition implies a perpetuation of needless mortality. In the past, and still in the poorer parts of the world, a great majority of children born have died before reaching maturity. All the waste and sorrow and pain involved in this mortality is unnecessary, and now that we know it to be unnecessary, those who insist upon perpetuating systems which involve it cannot be absolved from responsibility for all the suffering that their dogmatism demands. Nobody would defend such a wasteful system in the production of anything other than human beings. Suppose that bakers had for ages produced bread by methods which led to half the loaves they produced being uneatable, and suppose that someone discovered a new method, by which nearly all the loaves could be eatable, would it seem sensible to maintain that the new method was wicked, and that there is something virtuous about waste? And yet bad loaves do not suffer, whereas the wasted children die slowly after years of misery. Anybody who walks through a Chinese village, and sees the children with distended stomachs from eating earth because there was nothing else to eat, and who nevertheless feels that nothing must be done to prevent this evil, cannot be absolved of hard-heartedness. For if he were not hard-hearted, he would find the dogma compelling his cruel creed unbelievable.

Contrast with this misery the prosperous populations of the United States, Canada, Australia, or New Zealand. In these countries, certain ancient evils which have afflicted all sentient creatures since the dawn of life have been eliminated; no one need fear starvation; the great majority of children live to maturity; most people enjoy much beyond necessaries, and there is a surplus which makes it possible to give education to all. The old struggle for life is eliminated in its fiercer aspects, and could be eliminated completely if men would get rid of ancient beliefs, no longer suited to their circumstances. There is no good reason why a similar condition of well-being should not exist throughout the world. Certain things are necessary to this end: the birth-rate must be diminished; the land system must be reformed; there must be a measure of industrialization, and there must be education. But unless and until the birth-rate is diminished, no other measures give any hope of more than a brief temporary improvement.

It would be completely possible to make the whole world within fifty years as prosperous as the United States is now. It would be possible to lift from human life the ancient load of toil and sorrow. But if this is to be done, we must acknowledge that our power over nature has its limits; that we can without excessive labor produce enough food for a certain population, but not for more. It is probable that improvements in technique will increase the size of the population that can be supported in tolerable prosperity, but there must always be a limit, and when the birth-rate is excessive, population will press against this limit, and will only be kept from passing it by widespread unnecessary suffering. Propagandists have acquired a habit of talking about "Western values," and it must be confessed that a great deal of what they say is rubbish. I am inclined to think that the most important of Western values is the habit of a low birth-rate. If this can be spread throughout the world, the rest of what is good in Western life can also be spread. There can be not only prosperity, but peace. But if the West continues to monopolize the benefits of low birth-rate, war, pestilence and famine must continue, and our brief emergence from these ancient evils must be swallowed in a new flood of ignorance, destitution and war.

PART II

Man and Man

VI

Social Units

MAN is sometimes classed as a gregarious animal, but he is not quite similar psychologically to other gregarious animals. His gregariousness, when it goes beyond a very limited degree, is a product rather of self-interest than of instinct. Ants and bees instinctively serve the purposes of their group; they have no need of morals and decalogues, and apparently never feel any impulse to sin. Gregarious mammals are not so completely dominated by the herd as ants and bees are, but have less tendency to individualism than human beings have. In human beings there is a constant conflict between the individual and the herd, a conflict which as a rule is subjective, and waged in the mind of the individual, but occasionally breaks out into open disagreement. Every man feels himself at once an individual and a member of a group, and it is because both these feelings are so deeply engrained in his nature that he has found it necessary to make moral codes and prohibitions and a vast apparatus of praise and blame. Almost everything that goes wrong in the relations of man with man, goes wrong because the self-impulses outweigh the herd-impulses in cases where self-interest, or at any rate, the self-interest of the herd, would demand the opposite. The forms taken by this conflict depend, of course, upon the size and character of the herd.

53

The only social group that has a really profound instinctive hold is the family. Sexual and parental affection are part of the make-up of primitive man. Young children need the care of the mother, and while the mother is caring for young children, she needs the care of the father. The family is, therefore, biologically necessary to primitive man, and primitive man, just because he was primitive, would not have acted as biological necessity required unless he had spontaneous impulses to act in this way. For various reasons, men seem to have very early enlarged the social group to consist of several families and not only one. I do not know why they took this step; perhaps it was for mutual defense, or perhaps it was to gain the advantage of co-operative methods of hunting, or perhaps it arose merely through a habit of counting somewhat distant relations as members of the family. However that may be, man seems to have passed at a very early stage from the family to the tribe as the dominant social unit, and it would seem that as men advanced, the size of the tribe gradually increased.

Whatever the dominant social unit at any stage of social evolution, there were two opposite patterns of behavior: one towards members of the same tribe, the other towards outsiders. Within the group, co-operation was the rule; friendly feeling was expected and usually achieved. To this, however, there were limits, especially owing to sexual rivalry; if at any time the number of females happened to be less than the number of males, it was to be expected that there would be vehement combats between the males of a single tribe. Such combats would occur even when the numbers of men and women were equal if polygamy was tolerated; and as soon as tribes came to have chiefs it was to be expected that the chiefs would permit themselves many wives. This is one of the ways in which harmony within the tribe required the support of custom and the moral law. Within the family the same result had been achieved at a very early date by means of the incest tabu, and the various complex rules of exogamy which are common in savage tribes must have been intended to extend beyond the family the same rule of law that had been secured by the prohibition of incest. The incest tabu is perhaps the most successful example known of the victory of custom over instinct. The great majority of mankind at the present day go through life without at any moment experiencing any conscious impulse towards incest. There are, it is true, savage tribes where the impulse is still difficult to resist, and where adult brothers and sisters take pains not to meet. But in the main the prohibition has proved effective not only outwardly but inwardly, presumably because it is ancient and absolute and does not demand anything superhumanly difficult. To the social psychologist it is important, since it shows what custom can achieve.

Although rivalry within the group inevitably occurs, it is viewed as undesirable and as implying behavior deserving of censure. It is quite otherwise with rivalry between different tribes. Towards human beings outside the tribe, the normal attitude was one of rivalry in so far as it was not merely one of aloofness. So long as there was plenty of room, different tribes might avoid each other, but when, owing to food shortage, two tribes coveted the same territory, war was the almost inevitable outcome. In general, a war would be won by the larger tribe, and this must have led to a continual increase in the size of tribes. In difficult times there can, of course, be rivalry for food within the herd. In times of famine people will even eat their own children. But the emotions which they feel when they behave in this way are quite different from those aroused by war. If you are a cannibal, you eat your enemy whom you have killed in war with feelings of exultation and triumph; but if you are a starving peasant reduced to eating your own children, you do so with horror and revulsion and only under the stress of utmost need. Joseph Conrad wrote a story called *Falk*, which illustrates this type of psychology. Falk was a sailor on a derelict ship, where the food supply was exhausted. He and one other member of the crew alone had firearms. After these two had stalked each other for days, Falk succeeded in shooting his rival. After this he shot the crew one by one and ate them. Just as he had finished the last morsel of the last of them, he was rescued. When he relates the incident he says that it was most unfortunate for him, and that ever since he has had nightmares and been a vegetarian. This is very different from the attitude of the victorious cannibal in war.

As social units grow larger, the psychological mechanism from which they derive support is gradually diluted. Loyalty to one's family is a natural emotion. Everybody knows how in the middle of a family quarrel the disputants will instantly unite against an external enemy. A good deal of this feeling of solidarity can extend to a tribe, and can survive even into a fairly high level of civilization, as in the Scottish clans before 1745, or in Japan before 1868. But when tribes unite into a nation, the feeling of loyalty to the nation is generally, at least at first, much less vivid and compelling than the feeling of loyalty to the tribe. Loyalty to one's nation does not as a rule become a really powerful feeling until one's nation is attacked by external enemies, or at least is threatened with attack. It is still more difficult to feel loyalty towards an alliance of several nations. Such loyalty, where it exists, has almost no instinctive basis, and is almost wholly dependent on considerations of self-interest. That is why allies almost invariably hate each other.

A political organization, if it lasts long enough, becomes mirrored in the feelings of its members. The old mechanism of friendship within and hostility without adapts itself, with a certain amount of creaking, to the expanding political system. England and Scotland hated each other until the accession of James I. They hated each other again in the time of Cromwell;

but the Lowlands ceased to hate England when they co-
operated with the English to defeat the Jacobites. So long as
we have common external enemies, hostility between England
and Scotland will be kept within limits, but incidents like the
Stone of Scone show how easily it could break out.

Every new social organization tends to weaken the hold of
older organizations. This is especially noteworthy in the case
of the family. In the Bible, widows and orphans are regarded
as unfortunate because in the absence of a male protector they
are likely to suffer injustice. Modern widows and orphans are
in a different situation, since the State looks after them, not
always so well as the father would have done, but also not
always so badly. In the modern world the family consists only
of parents and children. Formerly in Europe, and still in the
East, the family consists of all the direct descendants of the
oldest living male. The head of the family surrounds himself in
one household with his sons and their wives and their children
and even their children's children if there are any. The wife of
the head of the household normally devotes herself to persecuting her daughters-in-law, and if she drives them to suicide,
no one is either shocked or surprised. This system breaks down
where the State is strong. Given a totalitarian State, one might
expect that ultimately the family would break down completely, as in Plato's *Republic*. What is true of the family is
true also of other organizations; all of them tend to become
weaker when larger organizations are set above them. But
sometimes the larger organizations fail to flourish, and cen-
trifugal forces prevail. This happened, for example, when the
Western hemisphere rebelled against the dominion of Europe.
It might be expected to happen if a premature attempt were
made to establish a world State. But those who remember the
collapse of the League of Nations, and are seeing before their
eyes the disintegration of the United Nations, have no need of
emphasis to realize this fact.

Social cohesion is only effective when it has a psychological counterpart in the feelings of members of the group. But whether such feelings can be created artificially by education and governmental propaganda is a question of great importance to the political future of mankind. For the present I should wish it borne in mind, but I do not propose at this stage to discuss it.

VII

The Size of Social Units

THERE are two kinds of considerations which determine the size of a social unit. The first is technical, the second psychological.

From the technical point of view, the most profitable size for a social unit is continually increasing as technique advances. The human psychology is always adapted to earlier times, and therefore frequently offers obstacles to the growth of social units up to the size that would be technically most advantageous. Of this there have been innumerable examples from the dawn of history to the present day.

Taking first the technical considerations, there is, at any given stage, an optimum size for an organization. If it is smaller, it loses the benefits of co-operation; if it is larger, it loses unity. Where Governments are concerned, the essential condition is that it must be possible to transmit orders and troops from the center in less time than it takes to organize a revolt. Until modern times this was a question of roads. The empire of Darius depended upon the great road that he made from Susa to the western coast of Asia Minor. According to Herodotus, a messenger could travel this distance in a month, and an army could travel it in three months. The size of Darius's empire was about the limit of what was then technically possible. When the Ionian cities rebelled, it was a long time before Darius got an adequate army stationed among them, and during all this time they could prepare to meet him. He succeeded in subduing them, but only with considerable difficulty. Roads remained the chief means of empire down to the time of Napoleon, or perhaps even longer if we take account of such instances as the Khyber Pass. The Roman Empire depended entirely upon roads. When it fell, the roads sank into disrepair and only petty monarchies were possible, except where Mohammedan conquests prevented the collapse of civilization. Napoleon's roads through the Alps were famous and enabled him to keep Italy in order. From the time of Darius to the time of Napoleon, Governments depended upon foot soldiers and cavalry, as nothing could go faster than a horse. The first great change was made by railways. Perhaps if Napoleon had had railways he might have won the Russian campaign. Perhaps if railways had not existed in the United States at the time of the Civil War the victory of the North would have been impossible.

The technical effect of railways in enlarging the optimum size of States was certainly enormous, but perhaps the effect of the telegraph was equally great. Owing to the telegraph, orders can be transmitted practically instantaneously, and what is going on in subject provinces cannot easily be concealed from the capital. It may be doubted whether the Indian mutiny could have been suppressed if it had come before the days of steam, but it would have been suppressed much more quickly than it was if there had at that time been a cable to India.

A much greater difference has been made by airplanes. There are now no two habitable places on the globe which are more than two days' journey apart. A journey from London to Sydney is now a no more serious undertaking than a journey from London to Edinburgh was two hundred years ago.

As the art of conveying armies by air develops, the few remaining barriers, such as seas, mountains and big rivers, will grow less and less important, and every sovereign State will be able to attack any other at a moment's notice. There is now no technical limit to the optimum size of empires; in fact quite the contrary, for the munitions of war become so expensive that only very large States can afford them, and the raw materials required become so various, that small States are necessarily dependent upon imports, which may at any moment be cut off. Another advantage of large States is that they provide great free trade areas. These, of course, could exist without governmental amalgamation, and would do so if men were rational in this respect. But, in fact, while a Southern Englishman will receive without horror goods manufactured in Sheffield, he will be outraged when he finds himself asked to buy goods manufactured on the Continent. But this brings me to the psychological factors concerned in the size of social units.

The psychological factors which we must now consider tend, as I remarked before, to slow down the growth of States, and often to defeat entirely the movements that technical considerations would demand. It is difficult to hold a governmental unit together by force alone. I will not pretend that it is impossible, for it has sometimes been done successfully. But it requires a great expenditure of energy on the part of those who exert the force, and unless they win over the subject populations, their dominion is likely to be temporary. It is true that subject populations often are won over. In the Roman Empire no one except the Jews showed any wish to rebel after the first few years of Roman dominion. The same was true of the empire of the Caliph. There were, of course, dynastic wars, but these had nothing to do with the sentiments of the population and were not intended to disrupt the State. It is difficult to say why this sort of thing happens much less in the modern world

than it did in earlier times. The great enemy of modern conquerors is nationalism, a sentiment practically unknown in
former times to all except the Jews. Consider such governmental failures as those in India, Ireland and Poland. When the
Macedonians conquered part of India, they established a Greek
kingdom which lasted for centuries, and, so far as we know,
they provoked no nationalist reaction in India. If the Romans
could have conquered India, we may assume that India would
soon have been as acquiescent in being part of the Roman Empire as Spain, Gaul and Britain were. But in modern times
conquerors have no such luck. The case of Ireland is even more
surprising, since there was not there any difference of color,
or any serious difference of race. When Poland was parti-
tioned, everybody except the beneficiaries was shocked, and
the Poles retained their national sentiment as well as their sense
of unity, in spite of the division effected by political frontiers.
Most moderns accept nationalism as a natural phenomenon
and do not realize how new it is. So far as the modern world is
concerned, it was perhaps invented by Joan of Arc, but died
down in France during the Wars of Religion. It flourished in
Elizabethan England, and its pernicious doctrines were never
more beautifully expressed than by Shakespeare. It had a re-
birth in France at the time of the Revolution, because it was
necessary in resisting reactionary opponents. Napoleon taught
it to the Germans and the Russians, Metternich taught it to the
Italians, and gradually it spread throughout the world. The
only force which now is psychologically capable of outweigh-
ing it is Communism, and even Communism has been defeated
by it in Yugoslavia.

The powerlessness of governmental propaganda when it
comes in conflict with nationalism is the more surprising since
Governments now possess powerful means of propaganda that
are new and might have been expected to be irresistible. The
press and the radio work for the Government wherever the

liberal freedoms do not exist. And what is more important than either is education. Every child during the impressionable years is exposed to a point of view which, whether avowedly propagandist or not, is always such as might be expected to imbue the child with loyalty to his Government. Where a State is a national State, press and radio combine to increase enormously the loyalty of the citizen beyond what existed in former times. It is only where a State is not national that these methods fail. The social cohesion of the large national States of our time is in its intensity a quite new phenomenon. I suppose that ordinary English people must have felt some satisfaction when they heard of the victories of Trafalgar and Waterloo, but nobody reading Jane Austen can find any trace of such a feeling, and it must have been very pale in comparison with the feelings that are aroused by modern important victories or defeats. There is no doubt that modern techniques intensify social cohesion very greatly where it already exists, but they do not seem able to create it where a contrary sentiment prevails, as in the case of Ireland before 1922.

The techniques by which national cohesion is generated are somewhat raw and crude. Falsification of history generally plays a very large part; so does the National Anthem. And there is almost always a pretense that one's own nation is morally superior to other nations. "Confound their knavish tricks, frustrate their politics" is the normal view of foreigners. Fichte says: "To have character and to be German undoubtedly mean the same thing." Modern Russia has perhaps carried this process farther than it has ever been carried before. We learn that Copernicus was a Russian; that it was not Vasco da Gama, but a Russian, who discovered the Cape route to India; that the law of gravitation was discovered not by Newton, but by a supporter of Ivan the Terrible; and that Darwin's ideas came from Russian sources which he carefully concealed. This sort of thing is, of course, absurd. If men were anxious to live

happily they would allow a committee of Unesco to pronounce on all such matters. Careful genealogists would investi-
gate the opinion that Columbus was a Russian, and the correlative opinion that Shakespeare was an American. Whatever
decision was arrived at by Unesco on these important matters
would be taught in all schools of the world, whenever the
subjects concerned were mentioned. Consider the Battle of
Waterloo. The French will tell you that Napoleon was on the
very point of complete victory, when he was stabbed in the
back by the wicked Prussians. The Prussians will tell you that
Wellington would have suffered a complete disaster, but for
the timely assistance which they were able to bring, in spite
of his faulty strategy. The English will tell you that the bull-
dog tenacity of the British would have indubitably worn down
the French attack, even if Blücher had not appeared. No English schoolboy is allowed to know Wellington's comment on
the battle: "It was a damned nice thing," or Napoleon's comment: "In war, the English always lose every battle except the
last." Every country teaches history in a manner which inclines the young to think that their own side is sure of victory,
and therefore to increase the proneness to war, which almost
always in any case exceeds what is rational. Nationalism is in
our day the chief obstacle to the extension of social cohesion
beyond national boundaries. It is therefore the chief force
making for the extermination of the human race. Everybody is
agreed that the nationalism of other countries is absurd, but
the nationalism of one's own country is noble and splendid,
and any man who does not uphold it is a lily-livered cur. It is
interesting to see the operation of this sentiment in the United
States at the present day. The Republican party is so ardently
nationalist that it has to vilify all other nations, even those that
are most necessary to the success of American policy. One
would have supposed, for example, that the co-operation of
Britain might be thought useful in the present international

situation. Nevertheless, I find American newspapers using such phrases as "the yapping Yahoos of the British Socialist Government." If the "yapping Yahoos" were not saints (which they are), such phrases might possibly cause them to have something less than an ardent love for Americans. This is as clear an instance as could be found of hatred overriding self-interest. The Republicans apparently feel that if America could only prosper by causing other nations to prosper, then it would be better to fail.

Nationalism is by no means the only force which limits useful forms of social cohesion. Consider ancient Greece, for example. Every State in ancient Greece, except Sparta, was divided between democrats and oligarchs. The bitterness of party strife was incredible, and each side was always willing to put to death large numbers of its opponents. It was also willing to form alliances with other cities in which the same party was in power. But at no moment after the Persian war had been won was Greece willing to unite as a whole. Although the Greeks were the leaders of civilization, and although they had a sentiment of superiority to the "barbarians," they fought futile wars against each other, and exhausted themselves to the point where they could be subjugated by enemies from without. The conflicts of democrats and oligarchs, which had seemed so earth-shaking, were smothered under the weight of the Roman Empire, and became no more than squabbles on parish councils. The same thing happened to Renaissance Italy, and is happening to Western Europe.

What is mistakenly called "human nature" likes somebody to hate, and does not feel fully alive except when some enemy is being injured. It is this way of feeling that has hitherto set limits to the growth of social cohesion, which is now an imperative necessity if the human race is to continue. The real obstacles to world-wide social cohesion are in individual souls. They are the pleasure that we derive from hatred, malice and cruelty. If mankind is to survive, it will be necessary to find a way of living which does not involve indulgence in these pleasures. If such a way of living is to be successful, it must not be merely through self-denial and self-restraint. It must be by changing the sources of happiness and the unconscious impulses which mold our moral phrases. It is possible, and in slightly different circumstances it would be easy, to live happily—far more happily indeed than anyone now lives—without malice and hatred and the desire for victory in disastrous contests. Men must learn to live in this way if science and scientific technique is not to cause catastrophe. But this subject belongs to the conflict of man with himself of which I do not yet wish to speak.

VIII

The Rule of Force

C O-OPERATION between human beings may be voluntary on both sides, or may on one side consist merely of submission to superior power. I observed once a pair of ravens in captivity. Their keeper gave them one large lump of raw meat to be shared between them. The male raven seized it, pecked savagely at the female if she made the slightest attempt to get a bit, and ate as much as his stomach could hold before he allowed his wife anything at all. By that time, all the juiciest bits were gone. This relation of male and female exists in many animal species, and existed among human beings until 1918. One of the most astonishing things about our time is the change in the status of women, which has spread with amazing rapidity throughout most parts of the world. In civilized countries, such co-operation as now exists between a man and a woman is apt to involve consent on the part of the woman, and therefore to be no longer an example of the rule of force. This is part of the general tendency to concentrate all use of physical force in the hands of the State. The superiority of men over women was based originally entirely upon their superior physical strength, which enabled them to claim superiority in every other respect, without effective challenge from the weaker partner. Gradually, however, it came to be recognized that force ought not to be employed by private persons in their private relations, but should be employed only by the State in accordance with the law. Women became emancipated from men in proportion as both became slaves of the State. This statement is too epigrammatic to be quite true, but it may serve as a slightly inaccurate condensation of the truth.

Social co-operation was originally based almost entirely upon force. This applied even to sex relations so long as women captured in war were made into concubines. "To every captain a damsel or two"—say the triumphant wives in the Song of Deborah. The co-operation of the damsels was presumably not voluntary. The relation of parents and children was also entirely based upon force, so long as the children were young. When the children were grown up, and the fathers decrepit, the situation was reversed. Some tribes sell decrepit fathers to neighboring cannibals, which saves expense. But in time fathers, while still in the prime of life, took steps to avert this unpleasant end; they instructed their children, while the children were still docile from powerlessness, in the virtue of filial piety. Confucius, as every one knows, makes this the basis of all other virtues. The Fourth Commandment embodies what must, at the time it was formulated, have been already a long tradition. But it has quite forgotten the original reason for the precept, which was to avoid being eaten in old age. It says, "that *your* days may be long in the land"; what it means is "that *our* days may be long in the land," i.e. that we may escape being handed over to cannibals. Filial piety is a good example of the way in which a superiority which is originally one of physical strength acquires the sanction of religion, and is thereby able to survive even when it is no longer sustained by superior strength. There is no greater reason for children to honor parents than for parents to honor children, except that while the children are young, the parents are stronger than the children. The same thing, of course, happened in the relations of men and women. It was the duty of wives to submit to husbands, not of husbands to submit to wives. The only basis for this view was that if wives could be induced to accept it, it saved trouble for their husbands. "The man is not of the woman, but the woman of the man; neither was the man created for the woman, but the woman for the man" (1 Corinthians xi. 8, 9). I defy anyone to find any basis for this view, except that men have stronger muscles than women.

The pattern exemplified in the case of filial piety has been illustrated in many social relations. When a warlike minority conquers a peaceful majority, it depends at first only upon superior strength, but it becomes a hereditary aristocracy, and invents some mythology to perpetuate its superiority. Sometimes the conquerors are descended from the sun, sometimes from other gods; they have blue blood; they have a sense of honor denied to the vulgar; their intellect is superior, and they can understand matters beyond the comprehension of common men; above all, they have a sense of honor which demands that they should instantly kill anyone who insults them. This is considered a great virtue. The remarkable thing is that conquering aristocracies succeed in getting these views accepted by their subjects. Every yokel used to touch his hat to the lord of the manor, and I am told that there are some out of the way places where this still happens. Just as the elderly father secures himself against the grown-up son by teaching filial piety while the son is young, so aristocracies, long after they have grown decrepit and could no longer defeat the plebs in fair fight, manage to cling to power and wealth by means of the religious veneration which they instilled in their great days. Kings especially used to be successful in this way. Kings ruled by divine right; they had divine right because they were the sons of their fathers. But if you go back far enough, you find some ancestor who had only the right of strength, and seized the throne by force of arms. It is amazing what a short time it takes for divine right to become operative. Charles I ruled by divine right because Henry VII had won the Battle of Bosworth. The military origin of social distinctions is a thing which those who profit by inequalities are very loath to admit. You will find at the present day in India many men who have resented quite justly the insolence that the British used to display in that country, which was based solely on military victory. But these same men often have no objection to the caste system, although that also has its origin in the superiority of Aryan conquerors long ago. An inequality which persists long enough becomes sanctioned by a halo of religion; but the English were not in India for enough centuries to produce this result.

Slavery has always been based upon war. A slave is either a captive made in war or a descendant of a captive. There were Negro slaves in America, solely because the white men were the superiors of Africans in the use of firearms. Like other social inequalities, slavery had religious sanction so long as it persisted. It was justified by the curse of Ham. Although Negroes in the United States are now nominally free, the social stigma survives. Why is it more wicked for a Negro to rape a white woman than for a white man to rape a Negress? Solely because white men are superior in battle. I defy anybody to find any other reason whatever.

Although the rule of force is not a thing to be admired, and although one must be glad when it is replaced by something gentler and less unjust, it has nevertheless had a useful part to play in the development of social institutions. Government is a difficult art, and submission to government is difficult except as submission to force. In the formation of communities, Governments imposed by force have played a part which seems to have been essential. Most English people at the present day submit to their Government because they realize that the alternative would be disastrous anarchy and chaos. But there were long ages during which people preferred anarchy and chaos, if they could get it. There were long wars between kings and barons in which, fortunately, the barons extirpated each other. In the end the king emerged victorious; people obeyed him because he could compel obedience. And so the kingdom acquired unity and the habit of obeying law. When in the course of time the kingly power was curbed, it was curbed not by a revival of anarchy, but by new forms of government. It may be doubted, however, whether a single stable Government of the whole realm could ever have been achieved, except by passing through the stage of royal power.

The transition from kingly power to democracy which occurred in England in the period from Charles I to Queen Victoria is typical of a transition of which there are many other examples. Wherever there is a social unit there is necessarily government, and it is the power of the Government which gives coherence to the group concerned. But when once the group has been constituted, no matter how, its form of government may change without change in the composition of the group. Very often the most difficult stage is the constitution of a single governmental group, and the subsequent changes in its form of government are very much easier. No governmental group can be constituted without some curbing of anarchic impulses, and it is much easier for this curbing to take place if it is only the weaker members of the group that are restrained, while the stronger members find such of their impulses as were formerly anarchic transformed into exercise of governmental power. Victorian children might not make a noise while Papa was snoozing, but Papa might make a noise whenever he liked. His impulse to castigate children who interfered with his nap would have been anarchic aggression if the family group had not existed; but since it did exist, it was a proper exercise of the duty of parental discipline. In this way, social groups could be constituted without much interference with patterns of action that had existed before the groups were constituted, except where the actions of the weak were concerned. Take, for example, murder. Where a region is ruled by a conquering aristocracy, it may be taken as a general rule that social inferiors must not kill social superiors, or even each other, but that when social superiors kill social inferiors it is a just execution. In fact, if the superiors are not too impatient, they can get it done through the operation of the law. Attempts to form new groups by purely voluntary co-operation usually fail, because whatever Government is constituted for such groups does not command traditional respect, and is not likely to be allowed enough power to enforce respect.

The most important application of this principle in the present day is to world government. For the prevention of war, the existence of a single Government for the whole planet is indispensable. But a federal Government formed by mutual agreement, as the League of Nations and the United Nations were formed, is sure to be weak, because the constituent nations will feel, as the barons felt in the Middle Ages, that anarchy is better than loss of independence. And just as the substitution of orderly government for anarchy in the Middle Ages depended upon the victory of the royal power, so the substitution of order for anarchy in international relations, if it comes about, will come about through the superior power of some one nation or group of nations. And only after such a single Government has been constituted will it be possible for the evolution towards a democratic form of international government to begin. This view, which I have held for the last thirty years, encounters vehement opposition from all people of liberal outlook, and also from all nationalists of whatever nation. I agree, of course, that it would be far better to have an international Government constituted by agreement, but I am quite convinced that the love of national independence is too strong for such a Government to have effective power. When a single Government for the world, embodying the military supremacy of some nation or group of nations, has been in power for a century or so, it will begin to command that degree of respect that will make it possible to base its power upon law and sentiment rather than upon force; and when that happens, the international Government can become democratic. I do not say that this is a pleasant prospect; what I do say is that men's anarchic impulses are so strong as to be incapable of yielding in the first place to anything but superior force. This would not be the case if men were more rational, or less filled with hatred and fear. But so long as the present type of national sentiment persists, any attempt to establish a really vigorous international Government would be countered by an irresistible propaganda: "Would you rather live as slaves than die as free men?" the champions of national independence would ask. In every nation in which there was a good hope of not dying, but living, as free men, this rhetorical question would be answered by a general shout in favor of dying for freedom. I will not say that there is no hope of a better method of ending the international anarchy; what I do say is that there is no hope of this unless and until individuals are much changed from what they are now. It will be necessary that individuals shall have less feeling of hostility and fear towards other individuals, more hope of security as regards their own lives, and a far more vivid realization that, in the world which modern technique has created, the need of world-wide co-operation is absolute, if mankind is to survive. Can a leopard change his spots? I believe that he can, but if not, terrible calamities must befall him.

Law

LAW is often represented as an alternative to force, but this is a mistake. Law is only a way of organizing and concentrating force and transferring it from individuals to groups, or from small groups to larger ones. In a civilized community it is held that force should not be employed by private individuals, but should be exercised only by the State in accordance with certain rules. These rules constitute law. There are always exceptions; a man is allowed to exercise force in self-defense; in many countries he is allowed to commit murder if he finds his wife committing adultery. In countries where white men hold power over men of color, assaults by white men on colored men are viewed very leniently by white magistrates. In race riots, such as one which occurred in Detroit a few years ago, the police exercised much more severity against colored men than against white men. In America some fifty years ago, if there was a strike in a mining district, it was quite in order for the sons of mine-owners to make an expedition, after they had dined, into mining villages, where they would fire at anybody who offered a good target; but any retaliation by the poor against the rich met with condign punishment.

Such instances might perhaps be dismissed from our consideration as extra-legal excesses, which might be tolerated, but only where the authorities showed a culpable laxity. What is much more serious is the refusal of Governments in many parts of the world to be bound by ascertainable rules of law in the exercise of the powers of arrest and imprisonment. Under the influence of the doctrine of the rights of man, the American constitution forbade the Government from depriving any man of life, liberty, or property, except by due process of law, and enacted further that any law by which a man could be tried must have already existed at the time when he committed the act which was complained of. The English nominally accept similar restrictions upon the right of arrest and imprisonment, but in practice they are very ready to admit exceptions in difficult times. In Ireland and India, when the English governed those countries, they infringed the principle constantly; India, now that it is self-governing, faithfully copies British practice in this respect. What the Nazis used to do and what the Soviet Government still does in this respect is notorious. But although in most countries at most times the rule of law is subject to limitations, it is, nevertheless, important, and governs a very large part of those human relations that are liable to give rise to disputes.

Law in origin was merely a codification of the power of dominant groups, and did not aim at anything that to a modern man would appear to be justice. In many Germanic tribes, for example, if you committed a murder, you were fined, and the fine depended upon the social status of your victim. Wherever aristocracy existed, its members had various privileges which were not accorded to the plebs. In Japan before the Meiji era began a man who omitted to smile in the presence of a social superior could legally be killed then and there by the superior in question. This explains why European travelers find the Japanese a smiling race.

It would be absurd and unhistorical to find fault with such

injustices in primitive law. If they had not existed, law would not have been respected by the strong and would, therefore, never have become firmly established. On the whole, at most times and in most places, a bad system of law is better than none. This is, of course, not an absolute principle; there are occasions when revolution is called for, and when it is worth while to go through a period of anarchy in order to arrive at something less tyrannical and unjust than what is being over-thrown. But these periods are necessarily exceptional. Where revolution becomes endemic, as it has done at times in some parts of South America, the results are apt to be even worse than those which flow from unjust laws that are enforced and obeyed.

Law, however, is not merely a means of regularizing the rule of the stronger. It is also a means of regularizing social relations among equals. For example, where there is a landed aristocracy, a man may wish to leave his land to his children and to feel that their possession will be secure even if he dies while they are infants. This is only possible if the power of the State is used to protect their rights, for otherwise they would suffer the fate of the babes in the wood. In such a case the law represents the wishes of the majority of the dominant caste, even where these wishes come into conflict with those of individual powerful men.

Apart from punishing murder, the most important function of early law is the institution of property. Property has, of course, a basis in what the seventeenth century would have called "natural law." A man's house, and the plot of ground round it which he cultivates himself, will be felt by the other members of his tribe to be his, and will be protected by custom even before it is protected by law. But it is a long journey from this primitive origin to the conception of property as it has developed in modern capitalistic societies. There are, broadly speaking, two early sources of property: on the one hand, the right which a man claims to the produce of his own labor, and on the other hand, the right to the ownership of land which he has acquired by conquest. In the course of time, the man who has only the former right develops into a serf, whereas the other develops into a feudal lord.

With the coming of machine production, these sources of property rights become confused. No man in a machine industry produces the whole of anything. Suppose you work on the assembly line of a Ford car. Who can estimate what proportion of the total car you have produced? Or suppose, to take the matter a little farther, you are a clerk engaged in keeping the accounts of the firm; no doubt you are an essential part of the organization which produces the cars, but there is no principle of primitive justice by which it can be decided how many cars ought to be allotted to your share. The same sort of thing applies to ownership of land. William the Conqueror gave lands to his barons by taking them away from the Saxon thanes. From these barons they passed by sale or inheritance, step by step, to their owners in modern times. When the industrial revolution came, it turned out that some of these lands had immense value, and others hardly any. But those that had immense value derived their value from labor and capital, not from anything done by the land-owner. In so far as the land-owner was able to retain political power, he continued to be able to exact rent, and even to make laws, such as the Corn Laws, which would increase the amount of rent that he could exact. But when he lost political power this sort of thing was felt to be unjust, and his income rapidly diminished. This sort of thing is very difficult to fit into the framework of primitive property rights, such as may exist in a semi-civilized tribe. Indeed, the whole conception of property is a muddle, due to the confusion of ancient traditions with modern technique. In the modern world, although there are still many forms of property which are in a sense "natural," there are many other forms which are created by law, such, for example, as copyright and patent rights, and all the immense complications of company law. Throughout the long evolution from Hammurabi to the present day, the law has always undergone such changes as would transfer wealth from the former possessors of power to the newly powerful. Does anybody suppose that Rent Restriction Acts or Workman's Compensation Acts would ever have become law except in a democracy? Everybody remembers that death duties on land, which are a form of gradual confiscation, came about only as the result of a first-class political battle. Property, in fact, is what the dominant political group chooses that it should be. At each stage, it seems to those who make the law to be more than this. It seems to embody either some natural right or some principle of justice. But natural rights and justice alike vary from time to time, as moral conceptions alter with shifts in power.

Apart from the merits or demerits of any particular system of law, there are certain services which law performs for the community. It diminishes the opportunities for individual violence, and substitutes for the personal interest of a single person the average interest of the group which holds power. As between the different members of this group, it establishes a kind of impartiality, since a man who has to appear in the Law Courts is no longer the judge in his own case. Moreover, as a rule, the law will concede some rights even to those who do not belong to the dominant group, since otherwise there is danger of rebellion. And law, where it has long been firmly established, causes a partial atrophy of impulses to violence. Civilized men do not so readily use physical force in arguments with each other as they would do if law did not exist. Murder and theft, being in general not advantageous to their perpetrators, no longer form part of the accepted pattern of behavior, and the impulse to commit them accordingly diminishes. A civilized man differs from an uncivilized man, not only in education and knowledge, but in his habits and impulses. For although there is in everybody a certain energy impelling action, the action which this energy will prompt depends to an enormous extent upon opportunity and the customs of the society in which the man lives. So that a given man who in one society will have vehement impulses towards one sort of action will never even dream of such an action if he lives in a different kind of society. Most civilized men abstain from murder, not by means of an iron self-control, but because the thought of murder never enters their heads. In this way, what has begun as the rule of force becomes gradually part of a man's character, and is no longer felt as a restraint upon his freedom. Law is necessary for the formation of customs which make social harmony possible, and social harmony could not exist without habits which lead to the absence of violence. We should, I suppose, all wish for the development of a society in which prohibition and force are reduced to a minimum, and in which people act spontaneously in a way leading to social co-operation. But I think the road to such a society must necessarily lie through the enforcement of law, since otherwise good habits will never be formed, and the possibilities which arise from good habits will not exist.

There is a conception of justice, which is associated in people's minds with law, but is, in fact, a very different thing. Justice is conceived by modern democrats in a way quite different from that in which it was conceived in former times. Plato's *Republic* is, in form, an attempt to define justice, and after an immense discussion, it arrives at the interesting result that justice consists in giving every man his due, i.e. what it is just to give him. This remarkable piece of work has been greeted by almost all Plato's successors as showing stupendous profundity; but if any lesser man had said it, somebody would have pointed out that the definition is circular. One could, of course, avoid the circularity by saying that a man's due is to be measured by his services to the community, but I cannot imagine how his services to the community are to be estimated. Compare a baker and an opera singer. You could live without the services of the opera singer, but not without the services of the baker. On this ground you might say that the baker performs a greater service to the community; but no lover of music would agree. The whole conception of desert, which underlies any other conception of justice than one of equality, is impossible to carry out in any systematic manner. In the past it has always been held that the more power you have, the greater is your merit. But this is a view which, under the influence of democracy, has been increasingly challenged.

But although equality is the main concept that modern believers in democracy use in defining "justice," there is always some admixture of the idea of desert. In fact "justice" is a concept as to which most people's ideas are in a considerable degree of confusion. Most people would consider that an exceptional degree of either merit or demerit justifies exceptional treatment. They do not disapprove of rewards for public servants who have performed some conspicuous service, and their belief that it is right to punish criminals is seldom based entirely upon a deterrent view of punishment. Ardent supporters of capitalism have even been known to maintain that businessmen who make huge fortunes deserve their success by the utility of their labors. This extreme view, to my mind, is not a very easy one to maintain. But, in general, it must be admitted that society gains if there are rewards for useful actions, and the opposite for such as are harmful. I do not think, therefore, that flat equality can be recommended; what can be said, I think with truth, is that all inequality must be justified by its useful effects, and not by some abstract concept of merit or demerit. If crime could be better prevented by rewarding criminals than by punishing them, I should be in favor of rewarding them. I could imagine a system according to which all convicted criminals were believed to be hanged, but were, in fact, transported to a delicious South Sea island, where they would enjoy idle bliss. Such a system would be deterrent without being vindictive. The only objection that I can see to it is that some enterprising journalist would be sure to unearth the truth. I cannot think it an objection that under such a system criminals would be happy; but for the need of deterring criminality, the happiness of criminals would be just as desirable as that of other people.

I think, therefore, one should say that the principle of justice demands equality except in so far as inequality can be proved to be socially useful. The world has not yet come anywhere near to justice, even in this limited sense. There are abominable race inequalities, of which the most noteworthy examples are the treatment of Jews and Negroes. There are still injustices to women, even in England, where the principle of equal pay for equal work is not conceded. There is still inheritance, which gives advantages to the children of the rich. In all such ways there are inequalities that cannot be justified on any principle of utility. Such inequalities may be condemned as unjust, and where law sanctions them, it should, if possible, be changed. This is not merely on the ground that, in the abstract, injustice is a bad thing, but on the more concrete ground that it generates resentment and promotes social unrest. Every approach towards equality, other things being equal, promotes social stability, and social stability is the fundamental purpose of law.

The consideration of justice has brought us almost to the subject of the conflict of classes. Marx, as everyone knows, thought that the conflict of classes has always been the main cause of social change, and will continue to be so until his followers are victorious, after which people will live happily ever after, as at the end of a fairy tale. Marx himself is not concerned with justice, but only with resentment. It is inevitable, so he says, that the underprivileged should be resentful and should be a majority—hence instability, revolutions, class wars, etc. The motive of the whole process in his system is not any positive principle of justice, but the purely negative principle of hatred. I do not think that out of such a principle a good social system can be created. As we have seen in Soviet Russia, when men whose motive power is hatred acquire authority, they still from habit continue to hate, and will therefore turn upon each other. The only possible issue of such a psychology is dictatorship and a police State. This illustrates the principle which Marxists are apt to forget, namely, that it matters not only what is done but why it is done, since all passions, good and bad alike, have a certain momentum and a tendency to self-perpetuation. "Ye cannot gather figs of thistles"; but Marx was not a reader of the New Testament.

Conflicts of Manners of Life

THROUGHOUT known history, every new kind of technique has met with vehement opposition, usually of a warlike kind. This is still the case in our own day. The earliest form of such conflict that comes within historical times is the conflict between agriculturalists and pastoral nomads. This begins with the Hyksos and their conquest of Egypt. For many centuries after Egypt had become a settled agricultural country it was threatened by nomad tribes on its eastern frontier; and when the Government of Egypt for any reason was enfeebled, these tribes became a danger to the civilized manner of life that the Egyptians had established. Traces of this state of mind are still to be seen in the story of Joseph and his brethren, where we are told that "every shepherd is an abomination unto the Egyptians." This does not mean only that they were afraid that the growing corn might be trodden down by sheep and cattle; the word "abomination" is a theological one, implying something wicked or horrible and not merely a nuisance. The nomads had a correlative, though slightly different, feeling. They felt that people tied to the soil and having to labor with bowed back through the heat of the day were somewhat contemptible, as compared to those who enjoyed the free life of the open spaces, and could move on, when they so desired, to fresh woods and pastures new. This feeling is not yet extinct; it survives in all those young people who enjoy "westerns" about cowboys. Imagine these young persons to grow up physically without acquiring mental maturity, imagine them poor and vigorous on the borders of a country that is rich and decrepit, and you have a situation which has reproduced itself time and again in human history. The most noteworthy example was when the barbarians destroyed the Western Empire, and the Arabs conquered most of the Eastern Empire.

As a rule the nomads are at first very inferior in education to the agricultural populations whom they overcome. But when, as is usual, the nomads are very much fewer than the people whom they subdue, they become a thinly dispersed aristocracy, and they find that their new wealth is more enjoyable if they adopt some of the arts of civilization. This happened, for example, when the Mongols conquered China. Kublai Khan, although his grandfather had been a ruffianly barbarian, was a man of the highest culture, quite capable of stately pleasure domes and the rest of it. Theodoric, king of the Goths, was not quite so successful an example of this process, for although during many years he enjoyed talking to Boethius, the barbarian burst out in the end when he decided to put the philosopher to death. The Arabs are the most perfect example of the process, since in a very short time they acquired much of what was best in Byzantine civilization, and preserved it throughout the centuries during which Europe was in eclipse.

The existence of warlike nomads on the frontiers of peaceful agricultural populations has had a great influence in retarding the growth of civilization. Until modern times, civilized people were as a rule not quite so good at fighting as uncivilized people. There were, of course, exceptions. The Romans could defeat barbarians who were less civilized than the Romans, but they could also defeat the Greeks, who were more civilized. Civilized life has at most times been insecure, owing to the risk of conquest by uncivilized warlike neighbors. Sometimes this has been a purely internal development, unconnected with foreign conquest. The Lady Murasaki portrays an exquisitely civilized society, in which a man falls in love with a lady he has never seen because of the beauty of her handwriting; but the whole of this was swept away by rough soldiers, who had vigor without culture. One of the great difficulties of the civilized portion of mankind in past ages has been to preserve warlike prowess, in spite of wealth and ease and a settled way of life. It is thought by some that modern man has solved this problem by the invention of the atomic bomb; but perhaps such a view would be unduly optimistic. However that may be, the conquests of nomads have never increased the area inhabited by nomads. On the contrary, they have led them to appreciate the advantages which an aristocracy can enjoy by means of the labors of serfs, and have, therefore, on the whole, caused an increase in the area devoted to agriculture. This is an instance of the fact that a technique which is more efficient from the point of view of production is almost sure to spread at the expense of one which is less efficient in this respect, even if, from the point of view of war, the older manner of life is more likely to lead to victory.

I come now to another kind of conflict, in many ways similar to the one we have considered. I mean that between seafaring peoples and peoples tied to the land. This is a conflict which has been immensely important in history. The Minoan Empire appears to have been based upon sea-power, and to have been in the end destroyed by pirates. First the Phoenicians, and then the Greeks, established themselves at favorable sites in the Mediterranean by means of sea-power. It is sea-power that is celebrated in the Iliad, as appears from the catalogue of ships. Passing over some twenty centuries, we arrive at the Norsemen, who were the terror of Western Europe for about three hundred years. They destroyed the civilization of Ireland, and gravely damaged the budding civilization of Yorkshire. They terrified the French and conquered Sicily, not to mention England. These men began as pirates, but as soon as their piracy was successful, they acquired whatever civilization was to be obtained in the countries they had conquered. I remember Baedeker's compressed history of the town of Bari. He says: "This town was completely destroyed by William the Bad, and rebuilt by William the Good." William the Good was one generation farther removed from the original pirates.

It has been normal for pirates to develop into merchants. This happened to the Phoenicians and the Greeks, and in later times it happened to the Venetians, though it must be said that piratical habits died hard in Venice, as appears from the history of the fourth Crusade, when the Venetians, by their monopoly of sea-power, compelled the crusaders to attack Constantinople rather than the Turks, on the ground that this enterprise would be more lucrative. The English are taught to admire Drake and the other seadogs of Elizabeth's time, but one gets a very different view of them if one reads books by Spaniards, such as Madariaga's book, *The Rise of the Spanish Empire*. One finds there that there were peaceful communities doing their best to live a civilized and productive life in a new environment, and that Drake would suddenly descend upon them out of nowhere and behave just as the Norsemen had behaved in the ninth century But the English, like the Norsemen of an earlier time, quickly turned from pirates into traders. Whether their civilization was better than that of the Spaniards is a debatable question. In California anyone who likes to moralize can contrast the surviving Spanish mission stations with the palaces of film stars. I think it is our duty to prefer the latter.

Seafaring and maritime commerce, in spite of their connection with piracy, have on the whole been instruments for the spread of civilization. Seafaring people come across a variety of different national and tribal customs, and thereby tend to acquire a certain emancipation from prejudice. Commerce as a means of livelihood has not only this advantage, but another of great importance, namely, that the roles of buyer and seller are voluntary, and the advantage of the transaction has to be at least apparently mutual. This gives commercial peoples training in seeing the other man's point of view, and practice in non-forceful diplomacy. The Greeks, the Venetians, the Dutch and the British have all exemplified the civilizing influence of seafaring commerce. But the connection with piracy makes a transition to imperialism fatally easy. The Dutch and the British both illustrate this. And trade may easily be forced upon reluctant people by means of war. Of this, one of the most disgraceful examples was the Opium War in China in 1840. We brought Western civilization to China, but its blessings as exemplified by the present regime in that country are open to question.

The forms of conflict which we have considered are now out of date. There are few pastoral nomads left, and private commerce is confined to a few backward areas. In the modern world there is a new conflict, having the same kind of intensity and bitterness as the old conflicts that we have been considering. The new conflict is between industrialism and traditional agriculture. In this conflict Europe and North America are ranged against Asia. Russia, in spite of rapid industralization, is the champion of Asia, and is presented to the inhabitants of that continent as their shield and protector against the rapacity of Western machine production. But in fact the position of the agriculturalists is, in the long run, hopeless. Military power in the modern world is intimately bound up with industrialism, and so, for that matter, is agriculture in industrial countries.

Agriculturalists in these countries can hold their own, and profit by food scarcities to get high prices. But agriculturalists in the backward countries have no such opportunity. Wherever Russia is in control, they are kept almost down to subsistence level. In China and India they are already at this level. There is a grave danger that primitive agriculturalists, wherever they survive, may be kept under by dominant industrialism. By means of the slogans of Communism, they will be induced to part with such little liberty as they possess, under the impression that they are securing emancipation. By the time they become aware of their mistake, armies, police and spies will have complete control over them. And if the Soviet system is neither softened nor overthrown, they may suffer centuries of impoverished serfdom. But such a system would be unstable, and would be faced by growing hostility from rapidly increasing populations. Some day the industrialists would grow lazy, and might be overthrown as the Egyptian Government was by the Hyksos. But these are gloomy speculations, and fortunately they are very hypothetical. What is not hypothetical is that at the present moment, in spite of Russian industrialization, Soviet power is based mainly upon more or less primitive agriculture, and is opposed by societies which, even in their agriculture, become every day more industrialized. This is a new conflict of ways of life, analogous to the two that we have already considered. Let us hope that it will not last equally long, or entail as great a load of suffering.

World Government

WE have seen that for technical reasons it becomes
advantageous that social units should increase in
size as technique becomes more elaborate. Marx
made the world familiar with this thesis in economics, though
even there it has applications which he did not think of. Commerce, so far as it still exists, has tended to become an affair
of trade between nations, in which the part of merchants is
taken by Governments. The economic links between an industrial and an agricultural country, for example between Britain
and Argentina, are important; and the fact that both countries
are sovereign States makes trade between them a prickly matter, tending to cause hatred between Governments and peoples. This, of course, is absurd. A butcher needs bread and a
baker needs meat. There is, therefore, every reason why the
butcher and the baker should love one another, since each is
useful to the other. But if the butcher is one sovereign State
and the baker is another, if the number of loaves that the
butcher can exchange for his joints depends upon his skill
with the revolver, it is possible that the baker may cease to
regard him with ardent affection. This is precisely the situation in international trade at the present day; and if it did not
occur we should say that mankind could not be capable of

anything so ridiculous. Economic interdependence is very much greater than at any former time, but owing partly to the fact that our economic system has developed from one of private profit, and partly to separate national sovereignties, interdependence, instead of producing friendliness, tends to be a cause of hostility. As economics everywhere has come to be more and more intimately connected with the State, it has become more and more subordinate to politics. Marx held that politics is determined by economics, but that was because he was still under the influence of eighteenth-century rationalism, and imagined that what people most desire is to grow rich. Experience since his time has shown that there is something which people desire even more strongly, and that is to keep others poor. This is a matter in which military power necessarily plays a great part as soon as trade has come to be mainly between nations rather than between individuals. That is why politics has more and more come to predominate over economics.

The advantages of increasing the size of a social unit are nowhere so obvious as in war. In fact, war has been the main cause of the growth of units from families to tribes, from tribes to nations, and from nations to alliances of nations. But it is beginning to dawn upon some people that although large units are a great help towards victory, there is something which is even better than victory, and that is avoidance of war. In the past, war was often a profitable enterprise. The Seven Years' War certainly brought the English a good return on the capital expended, and the profitableness of earlier wars to the victors is even more evident. But modern war is an altogether different matter. This is due in the main to two causes: one, that weapons have become enormously expensive; and the other, that the social groups concerned in modern wars are very large. It is a mistake to think that modern war is more destructive of life than the simpler wars of former times. The actual casualties in the past were often quite as high a percentage of the forces engaged as they are now; and apart from casualties in battle, the deaths from disease were usually enormous. Over and over again in ancient and medieval history, you find whole armies practically exterminated by the plague. The atom-bomb is, of course, more spectacular, but the actual mortality rate among combatant populations, even where the atom-bomb is employed, is not as great as in many former wars. The population of Japan increased by about five millions during the Second World War, whereas it is estimated that during the Thirty Years' War the population of Germany was halved. Broadly speaking, it is not in general the case that as weapons become technically more efficient, the mortality in war is increased.

There is, however, in the use of the atom-bomb and the hydrogen-bomb a new danger, a danger which is not only new in kind but greater in degree than any that has existed in previous wars. We do not quite know what may be the effects of letting loose great floods of radioactivity. There are those—among them Einstein—who think that the result may be the extinction of all life on our planet. Short of that, it may easily happen that large fertile regions become infertile and uninhabitable, and that the populations of considerable areas are wiped out. I do not say that this will happen if atomic energy is employed in war; no one knows yet whether it will happen or not. But there is a risk that it may happen, and if it does repentance will come too late.

There is an oscillation in warfare between the strength of the attack and the strength of the defense. The happy ages are those in which the defense is strong; the unhappy, those in which the attack has the advantage. There is always a danger in our scientific age that at some moment the attack may acquire a really disastrous advantage. Bacteriological warfare, for example, may exterminate the enemy, but would be very likely to exterminate at the same time those who had inaugurated it. On the whole, increase of scientific skill makes war more dangerous, even if at any given moment it does not make it more deadly.

Apart from mortality, there are other respects in which modern war is worse than most wars of former times. Owing to the increased productivity of labor, it is possible to set aside a greater part of the population for the business of mutual slaughter, and the dislocation of daily life is greater in a modern world war than in most of the wars of former times. Fear of atomic bombs has made it irrational for populations to live in great cities. Americans, who have room to expand, are seriously contemplating spreading the population of New York over a large area. In England no such possibilities exist, short of large-scale emigration. In the pleasant and comfortable wars of the eighteenth and nineteenth centuries, it was chiefly the combatants who suffered; now the suffering falls increasingly upon civilians. I am an old man, and I can remember a time when it was not thought quite the thing to make war on women and children; but that happy age is past.

For all these reasons, war is a greater menace now than it was formerly. The prevention of war has become necessary if civilized life is to continue, perhaps if any kind of life is to continue. This matter is so imperative that we must not shrink from new forms of political thought or from the realization of new problems which could formerly be ignored, if not with impunity, at any rate without ultimate disaster.

War may be avoided by makeshifts and expedients and subtle diplomacy for a time, but precariously; and so long as our present political system continues, it must be taken as nearly certain that great wars will occur from time to time. This will inevitably happen so long as there are different sovereign States, each with its own armed forces, and each the unfettered judge of its own rights in any dispute. There is only one way in which the world can be made safe from war, and that is the creation of a single world-wide authority, possessing a monopoly of all the more serious weapons.

If a world Government is to prevent serious wars, there are certain minimum powers that it must possess. First and foremost, it must have a monopoly of all the major weapons of war, and adequate armed forces for their employment. Whatever steps may be necessary must be taken to ensure that the armed forces will in all circumstances be loyal to the central Government. The world Government should proclaim certain rules for the employment of its armed forces. The most important of these should be that, in any dispute between two States, each must submit to the decision of the world Government. Any employment of force by any State against any other shall constitute it a public enemy, and shall bring punishment by the armed forces of the world Government. These are the essential powers if the preservation of peace is to be possible. Given these, others will follow. There will be need of bodies to perform legislative and judicial functions. These will develop naturally if the military conditions are fulfilled; the difficult and vital point is the placing of irresistible force in the hands of the central authority.

The central Government may be democratic or totalitarian; it may owe its origin to consent or to conquest; it may be the national Government of a State which has achieved world conquest, or it may be an authority in which each State, or alternatively, each human being, has equal rights. For my part I believe that, if it is constituted, it will be on a basis of consent in some regions and conquest in others. In a world war between two groups of nations, it may be that the victorious group will disarm the defeated group and proceed to govern the world by means of unifying institutions developed during the war. Gradually the defeated nations could be admitted to partnership as war hostility cooled. I do not believe that the human race has sufficient statesmanship or capacity for mutual forbearance to establish a world Government on a basis of consent alone. That is why I think that an element of force will be needed in its establishment and in its preservation through the early years of its existence.

But although force may be necessary at first in some parts of the world, there will be no stability and no possibility of a liberal and democratic system unless certain great causes of conflict cease to be operative. I am not thinking of the day-to-day conflicts that at present characterize the cold war, nor of the see-saw of power politics. What I am thinking of are matters in which, as things stand, there is a genuine clash between the interests of one part of the world and the interests of another. I am thinking of matters regarded as so important that each side would sooner fight than yield. For instance: shall Southeast Asia continue to be overcrowded, or shall Australia and South America cease to be white men's countries? Such really difficult causes of conflict center round three problems: population, race and creed.

I have already spoken of the population problem, but a few words must be added about its political aspects. Until it is solved it will be impossible to bring the poorer parts of the world to anything like the same level of prosperity as is now enjoyed by the richer parts, and until there is a certain economic equalization throughout the world, there will be causes of envy and hatred such as will make any world Government dependent upon continual exercise of force by the stronger nations. Such a state of affairs will be unstable and dangerous and harsh. It will be impossible to feel that the world is in a satisfactory state until there is a certain degree of equality, and a certain acquiescence everywhere in the power of the world Government, and this will not be possible until the poorer nations of the world have become educated, modernized in their technique, and more or less stationary in population. This, you may think, is a distant prospect, but it need not be so. Vital statistics in the West during the last half-century have shown what is possible, and certainly hardly anybody in the West would have thought anything of the kind possible in the year 1800.

The conclusion to which we are driven by the facts that we have been considering is that, while great wars cannot be avoided until there is a world Government, a world Government cannot be stable until every important country has a nearly stationary population. As this is very far from being the case at present, our conclusion may seem depressing. But there is another side to it which is by no means depressing. In former days most children died in infancy, mortality in adult life was very high, and in every country the great majority of the population endured abject poverty. Now certain nations have succeeded in preserving the lives of the overwhelming majority of infants, in enormously lowering the adult death-rate, and in nearly eliminating abject poverty. All this would have been impossible but for the fall in the birth-rate. Other nations, where disease and abject poverty are still the rule, could achieve the same level of well-being by adopting the same methods. There is therefore a new hope for mankind. The hope cannot be realized unless the causes of present evils are understood. But it is the hope that needs to be emphasized. Modern man is master of his fate. What he suffers, he suffers because he is stupid or wicked, not because it is nature's decree. Happiness is his if he will adopt the means that lie ready to his hands.

XII

Racial Antagonism

ONE of the most obstinate and difficult of the problems to be solved if a stable world Government is to become possible is the hostility which is apt to arise between different races. When I speak of "races," I mean genuine biological varieties of the human species, not divisions created by the accidents of history or politics. The French and the English fought each other for 750 years, from the Battle of Hastings to the Battle of Waterloo, but at no time had they any instinctive dislike for each other; on the contrary, between wars they traveled in each other's countries, and their royal families intermarried. The attitude of the Americans of English descent to the Red Indians was very different, as is shown in their saying: "The only good Indian is a dead Indian." No one tried to make friends with them except a few who were exceptionally Christian or exceptionally liberal, for example, William Penn and Thomas Jefferson. It is the kind of hostility that existed between white men and Red Indians that I want to consider, not the sort that existed between the English and the French.

As a political problem, the Indians of the United States are no longer important; the victory of the white men has been too complete. The native races of the Western Pacific also do not constitute a serious problem. New Zealand has completely assimilated the Maoris, and offers (I think) the only instance in the world of successful mixing on equal terms between two widely different races. The Australian aborigines are too few, and too low in the scale of civilization, to have much effect upon the social or political life of Australia. The numerically important races, at the present time, are the whites, the Mongolians, and the Negroes. The inhabitants of India are a mixture of Aryan and Dravidian elements; the Semites, both Arabs and Jews, are in some degree racially distinct from other white men. But the three great divisions—white, Mongol, and Negro —remain biologically the most definite and politically the most important.

The subject of race antagonism has a rather close connection with the problems of overpopulation. At present white men have most of the power, but the other races have the most rapid increase of population. Russia occupies an exceptional position; its increase of population is very rapid, and politically it is more on the side of the non-whites than of non-Russian whites. It may be maintained that Russia has merely developed a new and more insidious form of white imperialism, in which control is exercised through the Communist party, of which the government is securely Russian. But however that may be, it must be admitted that Russians have far less of white man's insolence than English-speaking people have, and that their intolerances are ideological rather than racial. In racial problems Russia is to be commended, and it would be a good thing if other white nations followed Russia's example.

Let us begin with a few approximate figures. White men number roughly 750 million, of whom about 180 million are inhabitants of Russia or her satellites. There are about 450 million Chinese, and about 80 million Japanese; the total Mongolian population of the world is about 550 million. The Indian

peninsula contains about 390 million inhabitants, who are difficult to classify racially. Of Negroes there are about 100 million, not counting the half-castes of North and South America.
Arabs number about 50 million and Jews about 11 million. (It
is estimated that there are about five million fewer Jews than
there were before the Nazi persecution. This illustrates the
importance of the race problem.)

The division of the world between the Russian sphere and
the American sphere tends to become a division between Russians and non-whites on the one side, and whites who are not
Russian on the other. This is not quite the fact at present, but
if the cold war continues long enough it is likely to become
the fact, at least approximately, unless on the Western side
very vigorous measures are taken to win the friendship of the
non-whites.

Let us begin with the relations of whites and Africans. This
has been, ever since the discovery of America, one of the most
shameful chapters in the history of nominally Christian nations. All the parts of North and South America that were
first settled were hot, and white men considered that they
could not be developed without colored labor. Red Indians
could not be forced to work, and therefore recourse was had
to Negroes. The horrors of the slave trade are familiar, and I
will not dwell on them. The life of a slave might or might not
be one of great hardship; as a rule, household slaves were fairly
well treated, but plantation slaves were cruelly exploited. The
slave trade was stopped at the beginning of the nineteenth century, and slavery in the United States was ended by the Civil
War. But the colored population remained, and remains, subject to intolerable hardships and injustices and cruelties, and
by the brutal assertion of their ascendancy white men suffer
moral degradation.

As the lot of the Negro in America improved, his lot in
Africa became worse as a result of the establishment of white

government throughout most of that continent. In the Congo, while under the personal rule of King Leopold II, there were large-scale systematic atrocities as dreadful as anything perpetrated by the Nazis or alleged against the Soviet Government by its bitterest enemies. In fifteen years this enlightened monarch, a pillar of the Church, and an ardent self-proclaimed philanthropist, reduced the population of his African kingdom approximately from 20 million to 9 million. At length, in spite of the vigorous support of the Catholic Church, he was deprived of his power, but not before he had accumulated a vast fortune out of the torture of black men.

In the French Congo there have also been malpractices, though not on the same scale. André Gide investigated them, and they turned him into a Communist; but when he discovered similar evils in Soviet Russia he was forced to realize that the problem of human depravity is more difficult to solve than he had supposed.

In the Dominion of South Africa, where a comparatively enlightened policy had prevailed, the present Government is engaged in reviving ancient tyrannies and injustices, although, by doing so, it is leading every educated Negro throughout the world to seek in Russia the only hope for his tortured race —tortured by the very men who proclaim their Christianity and idealism in opposition to the heartless materialism of the Soviet regime. Alas, the enemies of the wicked are not always virtuous.

As regards color prejudice there is a great difference between Southern and Northern Europeans. Southern Europeans may be abominably cruel to Negroes when it seems to their interest to be so, but they have no prejudice against them as such. White women have no objection to associating with Negro men, and colored blood has none of the social stigma that it has in the United States and in South Africa. The consequence of this is that in most parts of South America there are very few pure whites, and the color problem scarcely exists. Nordics and people of British descent usually maintain that the mixture produces a degraded population that is biologically undesirable. But as to this there is no clear evidence.

In the thinking of white men in the southern portions of the United States there is a great deal of confused passion. They view with utter horror the notion of a white woman having intercourse with a colored man; they state that colored people stink and are physically repulsive; at the same time they employ them as servants, and, what is more, the vast majority have an admixture of white blood. It soon becomes evident to the observer that the talk of Negroes being physically repulsive is humbug, and that what white men find unendurable is any attempt on the part of colored people to assert social and economic equality or to obtain justice in the law-courts. Nevertheless, it would be an undue simplification to assume that the feeling towards colored people has no instinctive basis.

Before considering possible solutions of the race question, let us continue our survey of the relevant facts. The set of facts to be considered next are the relations of white men to Asiatics.

The Chinese and Japanese are industrious and skillful workers, accustomed to a much lower standard of life than that of men of European origin. Given free rights of immigration and of competition in the labor market, they would soon oust white wage-earners in any country where they were tolerated. Originally, they were favored by Californian and Australian capitalists, who, if they had had their way, would have reduced the white population to a small oligarchy. Bitter resentment led, in California, to violence and race riots. In the end, owing to political democracy, Asiatics were excluded from both Australia and the United States. When I speak of democracy in this connection, I mean, of course, democracy among white men; world democracy in a world Government would have had an opposite result. Those who hold—as I certainly do—that it would be regrettable if California and Australia ceased to be white men's countries, must seek some principle other than democracy to justify their opinion. But is there any such principle that can possibly be made acceptable to Asiatics? And, if not, how should a world Government be constituted?

A very interesting example of race feeling arose in Britain on the question of Chinese labor in the Transvaal mines after the Boer War. Throughout that war the Conservative Government had asserted that, at its conclusion, there would be very profitable employment for British miners in South Africa. But when the war ended, indentured Chinese laborers were imported into the mines, and did the work for a small fraction of the wages that British miners would have demanded. There was a wave of passionate indignation, nominally because the imported Chinese worked in semi-servile conditions, but, in fact, mainly because of resentment on account of the displacement of white labor. At the next General Election the Conservatives suffered an unprecedented defeat, and they remained out of power for many years. The Chinese were sent home, but to a great extent it was Negroes, not white men, who replaced them. By that time, however, the British democracy was thinking of other things: the First World War was approaching, and more attention was being paid to the German Navy than to the Rand mines.

There is a quite different situation in regions such as Malaya and the Dutch East Indies. Here white people are bound to be a small minority, and the Chinese represent a higher civilization than that of the indigenous population. They arouse something of the same kind of hostility as is aroused elsewhere by Jews. And recently they have incurred the suspicion of the authorities because they often foment Communist agitation. But this is not a race problem in the sense with which we are concerned.

In India, so long as the British were in power, they treated all Indians as inferiors, refusing to admit them to white men's clubs whatever their qualifications might be. This was utterly indefensible. There is no respect in which a man such as Nehru is inferior to the very best of white men. British social insolence had a great deal to do with the opposition to British rule. All that, however, is now past history—happily. I think that, in historical retrospect, the greatest achievement of the present British Labor Government will be considered to have been the liberation of India without the bitterness of violent conflict.

I come now to one of the most singular, unfortunate, and beastly of race prejudices—I mean, the hostility to Jews. Originally the hostility to Jews was religious, not racial. The Romans, while they were pagan, were annoyed with the Jews because they would not worship the Emperor. When the Empire became Christian, Jews became the object of a much fiercer enmity because they had rejected Christ. But it was still open to them, as to Shylock, to escape persecution by becoming Christian. In the Middle Ages, economic and theological motives combined. The Spanish Inquisition, which was originally directed mainly against Jews, was content to accept conversion except when there was doubt as to its genuineness. But during the Crusades, when religious excitement led to many appalling pogroms, Christians ousted the Jews from their previous practical monopoly of trade. In England all Jews were expelled, and throughout Christendom their position was much worse after the Crusades than before. In Germany pogroms continued till the early nineteenth century; in Russia till 1917. What the Nazis did to the Jews we all know: they deliberately exterminated about five million of them, not for any crime, but solely for being Jews. The Nazi objection to Jews was purely racial and economic; religion had no part in it.

Let us now try to analyze racial antagonism, and for the sake of definiteness let us begin with the Jews. If you ask a modern anti-Semite why he dislikes Jews, he will tell you that they are unscrupulous and sharp in business and merciless to their debtors; he will tell you that they are always on the make, always intriguing, always supporting each other against Gentile competitors. If you say you have sometimes found similar characteristics among Christians, the anti-Semite will say: "Oh, of course I don't deny there are ruffians who are not Jews. And I have some very good friends among Jews. But I am speaking of the average." If you question him when he is off his guard, you will find that whenever a Jew engages in a bit of sharp practice he says, "how like a Jew," but when a Gentile does likewise he says "and, you know, the astonishing thing is that he is not a Jew." This is not a scientific method of arriving at averages. The fact is that attributing the traditional faults to Jews is merely rationalizing. They are thought to have these faults because they are disliked, not disliked for having these faults. For my part, in the course of very many dealings with Jews and Gentiles, I have found Jews at least as honorable as Gentiles in adherence to undertakings.

Why, then, are Jews disliked? Partly, no doubt, because they are successful. They are successful because they are industrious. But when we are beaten by a competitor we do not like to attribute our failure to his superior merit, so we attribute it to his unscrupulous methods, and thereby justify our hatred of him.

There are, however, more instinctive reasons for the hatred of Jews, and these throw more light on other race hatreds. Quakers in business are just as successful as Jews, but are not equally hated. The instinctive root of race hatred is the fear of what is strange. Ants kill an ant from another nest; pigeons in captivity will peck to death a foreign pigeon introduced among them. What is strange is incalculable, and what is incalculable may be dangerous; this is the feeling which has led men to look for scientific laws. The anti-Semite regards the

Jews as a sort of secret society, with knowledge and dark designs that they communicate to each other, but never to Gentiles. Chinese are supposed to be engaged in conspiracies of secret societies with vast underground power. Negroes have their mysterious bush-telegraph. All these are objectifications of irrational fear, and since they show a man to be a coward they lead him to become a swashbuckling militarist. If Hitler had been a brave man he would not have been an anti-Semite.

Color prejudice appears to be in the main a modern thing. The Greeks before Alexander had a certain contempt for "barbarians," but that was a cultural feeling, not a racial one. In Roman times there is very little evidence either way; no one knows whether St. Cyprian and St. Augustine were white. In the Middle Ages religious prejudices outweighed racial bias. The feeling in Shakespeare's time may be gathered from *Othello*. Although Americans do not like to think so, Othello is a Negro; Iago calls him "the thick-lips." It is true that he is always called "the Moor," but in those days black men were so called: they were "black Moors," which became "blacka-moors." People are shocked when he marries Desdemona, but not nearly as shocked as modern Americans would be. He is pardoned so long as the State has need of him, but as soon as the Turks are defeated he is superseded. One gathers that his marriage was objected to because Desdemona was aristocratic, not because she was white. No one objected to Pocahontas as a white man's wife; on the contrary, she was treated with honor. The feeling against Indians developed later, after white settlers had come into conflict with them. In Spanish America it never developed.

I think—partly from introspection—that the instinctive root of color prejudice is mainly fear of subjection to alien power. I have faced hostile mobs in England, but they did not cause me as much fear as the mere phantasy of hostile mobs in Japan. This kind of fear is ever-present in slave-owning aristocracies;

they know that servile insurrections may break out without warning, and that, in that case, terrible things may befall the defeated masters. This fear translates itself into hatred as soon as there is any sign of disaffection or claim to equality on the part of the "inferior" race.

There is, however, something besides fear of subjection in the instinctive part of color prejudice, and that is the repulsion towards what is strange or unknown.

The purely instinctive element in race hatred is a small item in the total, and is not hard to overcome. The fear of what is strange, which is a large part of its essence, disappears with familiarity. If nothing else were involved, the whole trouble would disappear as soon as people of different races got used to each other. But there are always excuses for hatred of alien groups. Their habits are different from ours, and therefore (in our opinion) worse than ours. If they are successful, they are robbing us of opportunities that should be ours; if they are unsuccessful they are shiftless vagabonds. The existing population of the world is descended from the survivors of many ages of warfare, and is instinctively on the look-out for occasions of collective enmity. The desire for someone to hate fastens on the little core of instinct in race hatred, and builds around it a monstrous edifice of cruelty and unreason. The difficulties of our time spring from the fact that such hostilities now involve universal disaster, not only, as formerly, disaster only to the vanquished. That is why it is more important now than ever before to achieve a degree of rational control over our destructive passions.

Race hatred in general has two sources, apparently opposites, but really intimately connected. There is on the one hand the wish to feel superior, and on the other hand the fear of being inferior. The natural man wishes to feel himself a fine fellow, and therefore has an impulse to despise any group to which he does not belong. Men despise women—for are they not incapable of reason? Women despise men—for are they not all just grown-up children? The English used to despise the French—for did they not eat frogs? The French used to despise the English—for did they not get fuddled on beer? So long as such feelings of superiority are genuine we can feel a kindly and contemptuous liking for a group to which we do not belong.

But when once the feeling of superiority becomes insecure, and is replaced, partially or completely, by a feeling of inferiority, a deeper feeling comes into play, namely the hostile fear that all gregarious animals feel towards members of other herds. Strindberg hated women because he feared them. Women whose interests are domestic have no need to fear men, because in their own sphere they reign supreme. But when feminists grew interested in politics, they were compelled to hate men, because in that sphere men had superior power. So it has been with slave-owners; if the slaves were content with their inferior status, their masters could view them with contemptuous kindliness, but if the slaves demanded equality they became alarming, and were therefore hated.

The causes of friction between different races are very various, and range all the way from blind biological instinct to a wholly rational appraisal of self-interest. The bad relations between white and colored people in the United States are mainly of the former kind; they do no good to anyone, and if colored people came to be treated as equals everybody would be happier. On the other hand, the fear of Asiatic immigration into white men's countries requires no reinforcement from instinct. Certain nations have achieved a higher standard of life than certain others, and while those with a lower standard remain as prolific as they are at present, their admission as immigrants would merely lower the standard of life of the more prosperous nations without permanent gain to the less prosperous. Hostility to Jews is wholly irrational. It has no objective basis, and it is contrary to self-interest; it caused the decay of Spain, and the defeat of Germany in the Second World War.

Unfortunately it is the more rational forms of race hostility that offer the greatest obstacle to world Government. But as to this I need not repeat what I said in previous chapters.

There are three types of solution for race problems. When I speak of a "solution" I mean any system, good or bad, which avoids such evils as race riots, lynchings, and massacres. The first solution is to avoid all geographical propinquity. The second is a rigid caste system. The third is complete equality, including free intermarriage.

The first solution, that of avoiding geographical propinquity, is that which has been adopted in Australia. In this case the reasons for it, as I have already said, seem to me entirely cogent. But it is not always realized—certainly it was not always realized until the Japanese were in Papua—that it is a policy which depends upon superior military strength. Those who wish to keep a country to themselves must be in a position to defend it. This means, in present circumstances, that the American bloc must be strong enough to deter the Russian bloc from attacking it. It means, further, that, if a world Government is ever established, it must not be a pure democracy, for obviously a world democracy would vote to end the white man's monopoly of certain prosperous parts of the earth's surface. The only way to meet this difficulty would be to make it part of the constitution of the world Government that there should be no interference with immigration laws. And this, no doubt, would be done if the American bloc were still powerful. In many cases, however, this kind of solution is impossible. The two million Jews in New York cannot all be sent to Palestine, and no sane person would wish to send them there. The world has to learn to live with an admixture of Jews. The same thing applies to Negroes in North and South America and in South Africa. Some way must be found by which Jews and Gentiles, Negroes and white men, can live peaceably side by side in one community.

The caste system offers a solution of a sort, which in antiquity often had a considerable measure of success. The relations of Spartans and Helots are a familiar example. When white men first conquered India, in the time of the Vedas, they established there the caste system which has lasted down to our own day. Although it embodied the insolence of conquerors, it was accepted. But when the British, after another white man's conquest, endeavored to establish themselves as a new caste superior even to Brahmins, they were resented—partly, perhaps, because they simultaneously taught Macaulay's liberal maxims, which were hardly consistent with their practice. In the United States colored people are still an inferior caste, as appears in the complete ban on intermarriage. But the caste system is repugnant to modern ideas, and in the modern world appears as a makeshift rather than a solution.

Where racially distinct populations have to live side by side, the only real solution is complete intermixture. This is objected to usually on one side, and sometimes on both. Orthodox Jews have a horror of marrying Gentiles, much stronger than any Gentile prejudice against marrying Jews (except among the Nazis). This is regrettable. It would be much better if the separateness of Jews came to an end, and people ceased to notice whether a person was a Jew or not. There is nothing against this except prejudice on both sides. Just the same arguments apply to colored people in the United States.

It is sometimes maintained that racial mixture is biologically undesirable. There is no evidence whatever for this view. Nor is there, apparently, any reason to think that Negroes are congenitally less intelligent than white people, but as to that it will be difficult to judge until they have equal scope and equally good social conditions.

The Nazis and their ideological precursors made a vigorous

propaganda for racial purity, but the facts are against them. The purest races on earth are the Australian aborigines, the Hottentots, and the Pygmies. All the historically great races have resulted from a mixture. The Germans themselves are largely Slav; the Russians are largely Mongol. All the Mediterranean nations are mixed. The British are a combination of Germanic, Celtic, and pre-Celtic elements. The Athenians were mongrels, resulting from a mixture of northern barbarian conquerors with the old pre-Hellenic stock. There is therefore no rational ground for objecting to interbreeding of different races.

The conclusion of this long survey is twofold. On the one hand, where there is as yet no intermixture, and two nations have very different standards of life, it is wise to keep them separate by immigration laws while doing everything to raise the standard of life of the more backward nation that can be done without lowering the standard of life of the more prosperous nation. This requires that, if there is a world Government, it shall not interfere with immigration laws, and shall not have the right to alter frontiers without the consent of the populations concerned.

On the other hand, where a population is already racially mixed, the only real solution is to regard both races as completely equal, to allow intermarriage, and to await the time when racial purity will have become rare and racial differences will be forgotten.

Race antagonism is an illiberal and irrational heritage from our animal past. It is difficult, but not impossible, to eradicate, as everyone knows who has kept both a cat and a dog simultaneously. It must be eradicated if the world is to have peace. And the world must have peace before the end of the present century if any part of the human species—white or black, yellow or brown—is to survive.

Ever since there was organized government men have perpetrated certain vast abominations—war, slavery, the subjection of women, the extermination of defeated enemies. Read about Saul in the Bible, read about Auschwitz in official reports, and fill the intervening centuries with similar ghastly horrors. In regard to some of these things there has been improvement. The subjection of women has ended among civilized nations. Explicit and acknowledged slavery has ceased except in Russia. Some nations, after victory in war, exterminate only a percentage of their vanquished enemies, and do this by what is considered the more human and decent method of slow starvation, not by the old barbarous method of cutting their throats in hot blood. But racial injustice, involving many of the evils of slavery, survives; collective hatreds survive; and war survives. War, though decreed by Governments, results from an accumulation of evil passions in many separate individuals. To stop war, we must not only work on Governments; we must cleanse our own hearts of the poisons that make war seem reasonable: pride, fear, greed, envy, and contempt. It is a difficult business, but if it cannot be achieved, the end is death.

XIII

Creeds and Ideologies

THE most bitter struggles between different groups of mankind have been caused by one or more of three differences: of economic interest, of race, or of creed. In the First World War only economic interest was concerned; in the second, economic interest and creed. In the third, if it comes, economic interest, race and creed will all be involved. In this chapter I wish to consider fanatical differences of creed as a source of conflict, first historically and then in the present day.

The word "ideology," which is now common, means nearly the same thing as was formerly meant by "creed." An "ideology" may be defined as a system of beliefs leading to a line of conduct, both public and private, and supported, whenever it is politically important, by a priesthood or something analogous. The word was brought into general use by Napoleon, who objected to what he called *"idéologues"* because in his day they were mostly republican. I shall use the word "ideology" as practically synonymous with the word "creed," but with slightly less implication of dogmatic definiteness. One can speak of the "ideology" of American capitalism, but it would be stretching the use of words to call it a "creed."

Differences of creed are not necessarily a cause of strife;

they only become so when they are combined with fanatical intolerance. Buddhism came to China and Japan peaceably, without disturbing the ancient religions of those countries. No one in either China or Japan thought that only one religion could be true. The Chinese came to believe in both Buddhism and Confucianism, the Japanese in both Buddhism and Shinto. In the Greco-Roman world similar views were generally held. The Romans identified their gods with those of Greece. Temples to Egyptian and Babylonian gods were built in Rome. The worship of Mithra was allowed to spread freely, and people who took to worshiping foreign gods did not on that account reject their native religions.

In the ancient world before the rise of Christianity there was only one exception: the Jews. The First Commandment says: "Thou shalt have no other gods before me." This was a new conception, inaugurated by the prophets. In their day it met with considerable opposition from the Jews, as may be seen in Jeremiah's complaints about the Jewish worship of Ashtaroth, but during the Captivity it won a complete victory. This intolerance (as it seemed to pagans) provoked hostility, and at various times the Jews suffered persecution, which never succeeded in changing their views.

Christianity inherited this theological exclusiveness from the Jews. Any concession to pagan worships was "idolatry," and was regarded as gravely sinful. The persecution of Christians by the Roman Government was caused by this exclusiveness, which was regarded as subversive, especially because it involved rejection of the divinity of the Emperor. When the Empire became Christian exclusiveness was carried much farther. It was not enough to be Christian: it was necessary to be orthodox, and to reject all the many subtle heresies that afflicted the Church in the fourth and fifth centuries.

Wars of religion begin with the rise of Mohammedanism.

The Moslems, like the Christians and the Jews, held that there could be only one true Faith. They were less intolerant than the Christians, but sufficiently so to make any genuine peace between Christian and Moslem States impossible.

All through the Middle Ages war was used as an ideological weapon. Charlemagne converted the Saxons by massacring those who showed a reluctance to be baptized. The Templars and the Knights of St. John fought the Moslems. The third Crusade turned its arms against the Greek Orthodox Church. Simon de Montfort exterminated the Albigensian heretics. Henry V and the Council of Constance burnt the followers of Wycliffe. In Spain the Jews and Moors were first persecuted and then expelled. In the Balkans the Bogomil heresy was rooted out.

But all these wars and persecutions sank into insignificance by comparison with the wars of religion in the sixteenth and seventeenth centuries. Everywhere throughout what had been Catholic Europe the religion of the reigning sovereign, whichever it happened to be, was enforced with such severe penalties that the great majority acquiesced. Both sides held that it is right to assassinate a monarch of the opposite party; Guy Fawkes attempted it on behalf of the Catholics, and Ravaillac succeeded. Charles I's head was cut off, and Cromwell's body was hung in chains. The Thirty Years' War halved the population of Germany, but made almost no change in the balance of forces. At length, in view of the inconclusiveness of the struggle, a few enlightened nations, led by the Dutch, discovered that it was possible for Protestants and Catholics to live peaceably side by side. English fanatics had fled to America to escape persecution, and were able there to perpetuate the evil practices objection to which had caused them to leave England. But persecution in America ceased towards the end of the seventeenth century, except in the comparatively mild forms in which it still subsists. In Catholic countries religious persecution persisted until the French Revolution, after which political passions took its place.

Some opponents of Communism are attempting to produce an ideology for the Atlantic Powers, and for this purpose they have invented what they call "Western Values." These are supposed to consist of toleration, respect for individual liberty, and brotherly love. I am afraid this view is grossly unhistorical. If we compare Europe with other continents, it is marked out as the persecuting continent. Persecution only ceased after long and bitter experience of its futility; it continued as long as either Protestants or Catholics had any hope of exterminating the opposite party. The European record in this respect is far blacker than that of the Mohammedans, the Indians or the Chinese. No, if the West can claim superiority in anything, it is not in moral values but in science and scientific technique.

In the Book of Judges it says from time to time "And the land had rest forty years." The land of Europe had rest ninety-nine years, from 1815 to 1914. True, there were several Russo-Turkish wars, there was the Crimean War, there were Bismarck's three wars, there was the Boer War, and at the end of the period there was the Russo-Japanese War; but none of these produced at the time any profound upheaval, and none of them gave rise to a feeling of general insecurity such as now haunts us even in our dreams.

I was 42 when this era of tranquility ended. All of us who grew up at that time took for granted, almost without conscious thought, that the nineteenth century had set the pattern for the future. It had seen great changes, almost all beneficent; we expected more changes of the same sort. The practice of toleration, liberty and enlightenment had spread with astonishing rapidity. Nobody thought of the nineteenth century as a brief and exceptional interlude between two dark ages. Looking back, it is clear that we ought to have foreseen coming troubles: overpopulation, the end of great unde-veloped food-producing areas, the bitter competition pro-duced by the spread of industrialism in a number of countries all avid for power, the intoxication caused by Western ideas in intellectuals belonging to countries with other traditions and other circumstances. All this we ought to have foreseen, but we did not, and so when war came we found ourselves in a world for which we were intellectually and imaginatively un-prepared. Our statesmen found old maxims inapplicable, but could not think of new ones. Blindly the nations blundered on from folly to folly. If we are to understand our own time, we must find the key to it, not in the eighteenth and nine-teenth centuries, but in earlier, wilder and darker epochs.

So far as ideologies are concerned, the troubles of our time show themselves in an increase of fanaticism. There was, of course, some fanaticism in the period which now seems in ret-rospect to have been comparatively free from it. There was fanaticism in the French Revolution, but it was in control for only about two years. There was fanaticism in the German resistance to Napoleon, but it seemed to die down after 1815. There was fanaticism on both sides in the American Civil War and in the struggle between Russian revolutionaries and the Tsardom. But except in Russia the fanatics never seemed to gain control for any length of time.

Since 1914—largely, I think, as a result of sufferings caused by war—we have seen fanaticisms of various kinds controlling governments and making sensible statesmanship impossible. There was anti-German fanaticism in the years after the First World War; there was answering German fanaticism, leading to the victory of the Nazis. There was anti-Semitic fanaticism, with the inevitable response of Zionist fanaticism. Most im-portant of all, there was, and is, Communist and anti-Com-munist fanaticism. While mankind remains in this temper, the sort of co-operation required for the inauguration of world Government is clearly out of the question.

The fanaticism which characterizes the Communist party at the present day arises from a combination of two forces: the doctrines of Marx, and the traditions of Russia. Something must be said about both. Before Marx, the leading Socialists—Owen, Saint-Simon and Fourier—were mild and philanthropic optimists, whose appeal was to reason and benevolence. Marx ridiculed these men as "Utopians." His own doctrine was fiercer and more dynamic. He did not expect or attempt to convert the propertied classes to his views. On the contrary, he held that, with negligible exceptions, men's political opinions express the economic interests of their class. Political divisions accordingly express the conflict between the interests of different classes. In the French Revolution the bourgeoisie had overthrown the feudal aristocracy; in the Communist revolution the proletariat would overthrow the bourgeoisie. The proletariat would be victorious because, by an inherent necessity, capitalism, as it developed, would diminish the number of the rich and increase the number of those who had "nothing to lose but their chains." The whole process, he held, was governed by a logical scheme standing above human volitions. If you were wise you would put yourself on the winning side, but it would win in any case.

The dynamic force of the doctrine, both in Marx and in his followers, was derived from hatred—illogically, since (in his view) the barbarities of the capitalists were fated, and were not due to their individual wickedness. His views were largely derived from a study of British factory workers in the early '40's—a horrible period, of child labor and famine artificially induced by the Corn Laws. Hatred was a natural reaction, but what Marx did was to erect hatred into a cosmic principle and the source of all progress. Naturally the propertied classes, wherever his creed spread, were terrified into violent reaction, and the vague good-natured liberalism of the middle nineteenth century gave way to a blacker and fiercer outlook.

There is in Marx a cold logic which is reminiscent of Calvin. Calvin held that certain people—chosen not for their virtues but arbitrarily—are predestined to go to heaven, and the rest are predestined to go to hell. No one has free will: if the elect behave well that is by God's grace, and if the reprobate behave badly, that again is because God has so willed it. So in Marx's system if you are born a proletarian you are fated to carry out the purposes of Dialectical Materialism (as the new God is called), while if you are born a bourgeois you are predestined to struggle vainly against the light, and to be cast into outer darkness if you live until the coming Revolution.

The whole process of history proceeds according to a logical system, which Marx took over, with slight modifications, from Hegel. Human developments are as irresistible and as independent of human will as the movements of the heavenly bodies. The force that brings about change in social affairs is the conflict of classes. After the proletarian revolution there will be only one class, and therefore change will cease. For a time the dispossessed bourgeoisie will suffer, and the elect, like Tertullian, will diversify their bliss by the contemplation of the damned in concentration camps. But Marx, more merciful than Calvin, will allow their sufferings to end with death.

This curiously primitive myth appealed to the less fortunate sections of mankind much as Christianity had appealed to slaves in the Roman Empire. It brought the hope of a great reversal, in which the oppressed would come to enjoy happiness, power and—sweetest of all—revenge. It should, according to the word of the new gospel, have appealed first to industrial workers in the most advanced countries, namely Britain and America. But in America wage-earners were always prosperous (unless they were immigrants or colored people), and in Britain the prosperity of wage-earners increased very rapidly during the second half of the nineteenth century. In both these countries, therefore, Marx won few adherents. He won many in Germany, but there, too, increasing prosperity led to a softening of the orthodox doctrine. It was in Russia, the most backward and the least industrialized of the Great Powers, that Marx's adherents first achieved the conquest of the Government.

When Communism became Russian it underwent gradually a very considerable transformation. When I was a young man I knew Bebel and the elder Liebknecht, who were the leaders of the Marxist party in Germany. Both were kindly humanitarians, psychologically very similar to other Radicals of that time. They did not hate their political opponents; they would speak of the Kaiser with good-natured derision. They felt convinced that the future was with them, but so did all the other reformers—the vegetarians, the teetotalers, the pacifists, the Armenians, the Macedonian patriots, and all the rest. This belief, at that time, was part of nineteenth-century optimism, and had not the character of a desperate revenge phantasy. The German Marxists of that time, of whom I knew many, were for the most part likable as individuals; one did not sense in them the vein of cruelty which has since become characteristic of Communists.

Modern Communism has been molded by two men, Lenin and Stalin. Lenin had lived long years in the West, and so had most of his colleagues. He wanted not only to introduce Communism in Russia, but also to Westernize the country. In this respect he stood much nearer to Marx than Stalin does.

Lenin was undoubtedly one of the most remarkable men of our time. His intellect, it is true, was narrow and second-rate; he could not think outside the framework of Marxian orthodoxy, and would consider a contention proved if it could be shown to be in accordance with the scriptures of Marx and

Engels. Where he was remarkable was in his inflexible faith and his indomitable will. Russia in 1917 was defeated and disorganized; the army had almost ceased to exist, the Germans held much of the country, and there were no forces capable of opposing their further advance; industry had collapsed, the peasants were in chaotic revolt, and various political parties were waging a bitter struggle with each other in spite of universal ruin. Lenin, immediately on his return from exile, marked out a narrow undeviating party line. First, with great difficulty, he persuaded the other leading Bolsheviks; then, by confidence and a show of inexorable logic, he converted the populace of Petrograd (as it then was). He won over the soldiers, who were returning from the front and refusing to go on fighting, by promising them peace and land. Within a few months he had made himself strong enough to frighten Kerensky's Provisional Government into abdication and to proclaim the seizure of power by his own party.

This, however, was only a beginning. The Provisional Government had decreed the election of a Constituent Assembly, and the elections were completed shortly after the Bolshevik *coup d'état*. When it appeared that the majority in this democratically elected Assembly were opposed to the Bolsheviks it was dissolved; from that time to the present the Bolsheviks have had no title but naked force to the government of Russia. Lenin's next step was to induce his colleagues, with great difficulty, to accept a humiliating peace with Germany. No sooner was this concluded than a civil war broke out, in which defeat often seemed imminent. America, Britain, France and Japan, as soon as they had defeated the Germans, sent troops to help the opponents of the Bolsheviks in the civil war. Nevertheless the Bolsheviks won, and the world had to acquiesce while they consolidated their power. Throughout the first two years or more the Bolsheviks themselves expected defeat, and the rest of the world was confident that they would fall, but they survived, and set to work to organize Russia in accordance with Marxian theory.

Russia, however, was very different from Western countries, and what emerged was not quite what Marx had had in mind. Russia was largely illiterate; the immense majority of the population were peasants; the Tsarist autocracy had accustomed people to autocratic government; the Church was more subservient to the State than in Western countries; superstition was as widespread as it had been in Western Europe in the Middle Ages. These things facilitated what was called the dictatorship of the proletariat, which was in fact the dictatorship of the inner ring of the Communist party. Lenin had always been ruthless, and the experiences of the civil war did not make him less so. The dangers of the situation hastened the return to autocracy and the police State, to which the country had been accustomed before the Revolution.

Russia had always been prone to fanaticism. There were many heretical sects which heroically endured persecution. Ivan the Terrible and Peter the Great were fanatics. The anarchist leader Bakunin was much more fanatical than Marx. The reactionaries who supported the Tsarist Government paved the way to their own downfall by fanatical resistance to modern ideas; down to 1917 even the mildest liberalism led to Siberia. The atmosphere of fanaticism survived the Revolution, and was if anything intensified by precarious success.

With the coming of Stalin the Soviet regime entered upon a new phase. Lenin was a cosmopolitan, who had lived in Western countries and had no special feeling for Russia. Stalin knew only Russia, and had no respect for the West. He liquidated the old Bolsheviks, and invoked traditional Russian patriotism to help out the Communist ideology. Just as, in Elizabethan England, patriotism went hand in hand with Protestantism, so in Stalin's Russia patriotism goes hand in hand with

Communism. Since most Russians are intensely patriotic, this gives great added strength to the regime. It must be acknowledged that Russia under Stalin has had amazing success. Communism is now in control in China, the Balkans, Poland and a large part of Germany, and there is every reason to expect further accessions of territory in Asia.

No success since the rise of Islam has been so rapid or so astonishing as the success of Communism. It is no wonder if the rest of the world is asking itself whether any limits short of the whole planet can be put to Soviet conquests.

Ten years ago another fanatical ideology, Fascism, seemed almost as threatening as Communism does now. Fascism has now gone underground, but perhaps only temporarily. At any rate the fanatical disposition which produced it is ready to be called out by the same kind of circumstances. The Nazis got their hold on Germany owing to the misery produced by the great depression, which, itself, was caused by the fanatical folly of American reactionaries. If America were again to pursue as mad an economic policy as that of the '20's, it is by no means impossible that correlative follies would again be generated in other countries.

Fanaticism in control of a Government is dangerous because it finds co-operation with others scarcely possible. Nazis and Communists alike have made treaties and agreements seem useless to the outside world, because their fanaticism makes them incapable of good faith. As things stand, a world Government is not possible unless Communism is overthrown or conquers the whole world. We must hope that its fanaticism will lessen, and that the hostile fanaticism of the United States will not meanwhile develop into an equal obstacle to co-operation.

Let us consider in a more general manner the nature of fanaticism, its causes, and the possible ways of diminishing it. The essence of fanaticism consists in regarding some one matter as so important as to outweigh everything else. The

Byzantines, in the last days before the Turkish conquest, thought it more important to avoid unleavened bread in the communion service than to preserve Constantinople for Christendom. A large proportion of the inhabitants of the Indian peninsula are willing to bring their country to ruin on the question whether the eating of pork or the eating of beef is the more abhorrent sin. American reactionaries would rather lose the next war than employ in atomic research anyone whose second cousin once met a Communist at a party. During the First World War Scottish Sabbatarians, in spite of the food shortage caused by German submarines, protested against the planting of potatoes on Sundays, and maintained that Divine wrath at this sin explained our lack of military success. Those who have theological objections to birth control are willing that destitution, famine and war shall continue till the end of time because they cannot forget one misinterpreted text in Genesis. The ardent friends and the bitter enemies of Communism are alike willing to see the human race radioactively exterminated rather than compromise with the evil thing— capitalism or Communism as the case may be. All these are examples of fanaticism.

In every community there is a certain percentage of temperamental fanatics. Some fanaticisms are essentially harmless, and others do no harm so long as their adherents are few and not in power. The Amish in Pennsylvania hold that it is wicked to use buttons; this is completely harmless except in so far as it shows an irrational state of mind. Some extreme Protestants would like to revive the persecution of Catholics; these people are only harmless so long as they are very few. Fanaticism only becomes a serious menace when some fanatical creed is held by a sufficient number of people to endanger the peace, either internally by civil war or externally by a crusade, or when, without civil war, it establishes a Rule of the Saints involving persecution and mental stagnation. Of this last the greatest example in history is the rule of the Church from the fourth century to the sixteenth. The greatest example in our time is the rule of the Communist Church, as it may be called.

Historically, the main causes of fanaticism have been misfortune and poverty. Fanaticism among Jews became common during the Babylonian captivity; it was promoted by persecution in the time of Antiochus IV and the Maccabees, and again after the destruction of Jerusalem; in our time, the fanaticism of the Nazis has, as was inevitable, generated a counter-fanaticism among a certain number of Jews. In Mohammedan countries, where Jews were well treated, they were never fanatics.

The fanaticism of the Nazis only became tolerable to ordinary Germans as a result of the poverty and humiliation brought about by the Treaty of Versailles and the great depression.

The fanaticism of Russian revolutionaries was caused by Tsarist persecution; in particular, Lenin's fanaticism was first generated by his brother's execution. In 1917, defeat in war, chaos, and ruin produced in large sections of the Russian population a proneness to fanaticism and a readiness to follow any leader who knew his own mind and was genuinely convinced that he could lead the way to salvation. After the Bolsheviks had broken with democracy by dismissing the Constituent Assembly, self-preservation and lust for power were added to fanaticism. These motives, which exist also in rich imperialist nations, have a causation different from that of fanaticism. This makes a difficulty in dealing with Russia, where both kinds of motives co-exist.

To cure fanaticism, except as a rare aberration of eccentric individuals, three things are needed: security, prosperity and a liberal education.

Lack of security exists throughout the world at the present time. We have all been told horrors about hydrogen-bombs and bacteriological war; we all know that war may break out at any moment. The atmosphere of terror is driving men into superstition, and into forms of intolerance which intensify the danger instead of diminishing it. If fanaticism is to grow less, whether in Russia or elsewhere, the first step must be to find some way of diminishing insecurity. This is difficult in the present state of world politics, but it must be done if disaster is to be averted.

Prosperity is generally admitted in the West to be the best preventive of Communist fanaticism, but no one seems to draw the conclusion that it would be a good thing if Russia were prosperous. Trade across the Iron Curtain ought to be encouraged. Everything possible should be done to turn the attention of Russians to the internal development of their own country. I admit that the Russians make these things difficult, but it is bound to take time and patience to dispel their suspicions.

Liberal education is the most difficult to secure of our three requisites. Russians will have none of it; the United States has less of it year by year. Consider the case of Dr. Lattimore, who was accused of being a traitor for saying things about China which every well-informed person knew to be true, and which it was to America's interest to have known by those who make American policy. In this respect matters will not improve until there is more sense of security, at least for a few years ahead. To create such a sense, on both sides of the Iron Curtain, is the main duty of statesmen in our time.

But how is this to be done? There must be a change of emphasis: we must devote ourselves to showing, not how to secure victory for our side, nor how desirable our victory would be, but how disastrous to everybody on all sides a war must be. In the West, where free discussion is possible, important men, especially scientists, of all shades of political opinion, should meet together. It should be agreed that never, in their discussions, must anyone raise the question as to which system is best, the Russian or the American. What should be made clear is: first, that if there is a war, then even if one side is completely victorious (which is unlikely) the victors will still be worse off than if there had been no war; second, that there is no reason, except mutual suspicion, why the two kinds of regime should not exist peaceably side by side; third, that it is possible to divide the world into spheres, leaving each side free in its own sphere, but agreeing not to interfere in the other. If in the West men of sufficient importance and sufficient political diversity, including Communists, had agreed on such a solution, it is not irrational to hope that Governments, on both sides of the Iron Curtain, would examine the proposals carefully, and would perhaps reach a basis of agreement. The alternative is disaster, not to this or that group, but to mankind.

If once the fear of imminent war were removed, I do not doubt that there would be a very rapid improvement. Russia would grow less illiberal, and the growth of intolerance in the United States would be checked.

World government, I repeat, must be our goal. I have dealt as candidly as I am able to do with the difficulties of population, of race, and of creed. I do not think these difficulties can be overcome in less than fifty years. Meanwhile the peace of the world must be preserved somehow by expedients and makeshifts and a general realization of what is at stake for mankind. The world has to learn economic common sense; different races have to treat each other as equals; and there must be tolerance as regards differences of creed. If there is no great war, natural tendencies will probably promote these things. And if, at last, it becomes possible to create a stable world Government, mankind may enter upon a period of prosperity and well-being without parallel in the past history of our species.

XIV

Economic Co-operation and Competition

HE science of economics has been wrapped around by the theorists in a series of many veils, which have caused the plain man to suppose that there must be something indecent about its naked form. I think the only thing to do in view of this situation is to begin again at the beginning with matters of such simplicity that the reader may be indignant at finding them mentioned, under the impression that I am deliberately insulting his intelligence. I can only assure him most solemnly that nothing is farther from my intentions.

Economics, as a subject distinct from military strategy, depends upon law. Its dependence upon law is very much greater than the classical economists realized. Let us, however, begin by ignoring the part played by law.

If you are a member of a primitive community and you wish to produce, say, food, there are two things that you must do: on the one hand, you must keep competitors off your land, and on the other hand you must compel your wife to work for you during the part of the day when it is so hot that you find work unpleasant. While you keep others off your land, you are the embryo of the military might of the State; while you make your wife work, you are the embryo of the capitalist. Your relation to your enemy is one of competition, whereas your relation to your wife is one of co-operation.

In an orderly community which is still at an early stage of economic development, for example, a village community in India or China, these matters are not left to the individual peasant. Law regulates the ownership of land, and custom, to some degree reinforced by law, regulates the economic relation of husband and wife. Competition in a primitive form of contest for the ownership of land becomes the prerogative of the State and is conducted by armies. Co-operation at this stage, as earlier, is almost confined within the family. The peasant raises his own food, with the exception of a few items such as salt and sugar. His tools are very simple and his clothing very inexpensive. His economic relations with the outside world, whether as buyer or seller, are therefore not very important. In the main, like a wild animal, he is a self-subsisting unit, or at any rate his family is. Neither competition nor co-operation in their important forms enter into his economic life.

"Competition" in the sense in which it is used in classical economics depends upon the existence of commerce regulated by law. It has, in theory, nothing to do with that more primitive competition which has become the function of armies, and which decides the ownership of land. It exists in theory only within a fixed framework of law. Given a number of men who all independently produce a certain commodity and expect to live by exchanging it for other commodities, they will obviously all try to get as much of other commodities in exchange as they can. But each will be limited in his demands by the fact that his competitor may ask less. This limitation only arises when the producers of the commodity in question between them can produce more of the commodity than can be sold at a profit, or at any rate without loss. The whole system only works where there are law-courts and policemen to enforce contracts. And as soon as the stage of primitive barter has been surpassed, there must also be a more or less stable currency which is legal tender. There are all kinds of elaborate legal restrictions of methods of competition. You must not assassinate your leading competitor; this form of competition is the prerogative of the State. You are allowed to tell the public how good your product is, but you must not tell them how bad the other man's is. At the same time, if you were to find out that the other man is guilty of an offense against morals, you would be entirely within your rights in giving publicity to the fact, unless it could be proved that you were actuated by malice. You, of course, would claim that you had acted solely from a desire to protect public virtue, and that the fact that the sinner happened to be your competitor had nothing to do with your action. This issue would be decided by a jury. Nevertheless, the classical economists describe such competition as "free."

All sorts of wonderful things were thought to result from "free" competition. It was thought that at a given price the better commodity would get the larger sales, and it was thought that any improvement in methods of production would enable the man who made the improvement to undersell his competitors. Thus competition would result in improving quality and cheapening methods of production. There may possibly have been some small element of truth in this theory 150 years ago in the cotton trade. Certainly the production of wage-earners was cheapened to the utmost, and so was the production of raw cotton by means of plantation slavery. The system worked admirably, except for the cotton operatives and the plantation slaves; but they did not write the economic textbooks.

But gradually things ceased to work out as the classical economists had supposed, though it was a long time before economists noticed this. Everybody except the consumer began to discover the advantages of combination. Manufacturers combined to avoid cut-throat competition with each other. Trade unions were formed to extend the advantages of combination to wage-earners. But this was thought shocking, since it interfered with the godlike principle of free competition. It was only after a long and bitter struggle that wage-earners acquired free rights of combination. In some industries it was found that possession of the raw material could give the power of monopoly, if it was skillfully employed. Railways, except in regard to certain points, were legally constituted monopolies. The power which this gave them is vividly portrayed in Norris's *Octopus*. Marx had foretold that free competition among capitalists would issue in monopoly, and this was found to be true when Rockefeller acquired a virtual monopoly of oil. The devotees of free competition were shocked and made laws to disrupt his monopoly. But it is difficult to compel people to fight when they would rather not, and anti-trust legislation in America, after a number of immensely expensive and ineffectual suits against monopolies, scored only one victory—Eugene V. Debs, the labor agitator, was sent to prison. This was not quite what had been intended by those who agitated against the Standard Oil Company and the Steel Trust.

Competition within a country belongs to an early stage of industrial development. In all the more important industries the tendency towards virtual monopoly is irresistible, and there comes a moment when either the industries take over the State, or the State takes over the industries. The former course is favored by those nostalgic devotees of the past who imagine that they are thereby serving the god of free competition. But the other course is the one which is increasingly being adopted in practice, even where in theory it is being avoided. Consequently, competition in the modern world is between nations, not between individual producers. The British, for instance, wish to sell motor-cars in America; this is a governmental matter to be decided between Whitehall and Washington. Whitehall has to decide how much in the way of raw materials can be allocated to the manufacture of motor-cars, and Washington has to consider how much irritation in Detroit is less harmful to the United States than the bankruptcy of the British Government. If the British were too successful in the export of cars, the American Government would raise the tariff. If they were too unsuccessful, it might conceivably suggest lowering the tariff. This sort of thing is a very long way from the free competition of the classical economists. I will not say that free competition no longer exists at all, for at certain levels it can still be found. If a schoolboy gets a postage stamp from Bali, those of his school-fellows who go in for stamp-collecting may compete freely in offers to buy it from him. But in more advanced economic operations, competition is not between individuals, but between States, and is subject to every kind of political consideration.

Modern industrial technique has made competition far less important than it used to be, and has made different industries and different parts of the world far more interdependent than they formerly were. The emphasis upon competition has led many people to suppose that whatever is disadvantageous to A must be advantageous to B. This comes of thinking that competition is a more fundamental and more frequent economic relation than co-operation. But such a view is completely out of date, and where it persists, it is very harmful.

Economic co-operation has two main forms: one is exchange, and the other is the fitting together of different stages in the production of one commodity. It should be fairly easy to understand that if you ruin your customer, he will not buy as much from you as he did when he was prosperous. But although this should be easy to understand, it seems that only a small minority of mankind are capable of such an effort of thought. Most people who are customers are also competitors, and if you are in business, you are more vividly conscious of them as competitors than as customers. Americans are annoyed when they find that if the British cannot earn dollars, they will buy less food and tobacco from America, because it faces them with a dilemma which is emotionally painful. Either the British must be prosperous, or certain large American interests must suffer. It is difficult to decide which is the more distressing alternative. This dilemma naturally stimulates anti-British sentiment in the United States.

The other modern form of co-operation, namely that between different stages in the production of a given commodity, is more interesting and more complex in its workings. Modern industrial technique requires a great deal of very expensive fixed capital which is only capable of certain uses. If the finished product which it is intended for is no longer in demand, this fixed capital becomes useless, and all the labor that has gone into producing it does nothing to increase the amount of consumable commodities. The same thing can happen at a more primitive level. If you plow a field and are then prevented from sowing the seed, your plowing has been wasted labor. If you sow the seed and bad weather prevents a harvest, your labor has again been wasted. But in the elaborate processes of modern machine production, there is a great deal more of this sort of thing. Modern methods are very much quicker than old methods in producing a great quantity of some commodity, but in general they are slower in producing a little of it. When Orellana wanted to descend the Amazon, he and his companions made a boat in a day or two which transported them successfully from near the source to the mouth of that river. When the United States Government desired a large number of ships to make good the depredations of U-boats during the Second World War, it was a long time before even one ship was produced, but as soon as one ship could be produced, a very large number could be produced in rapid succession. Modern methods of mass production require an immense amount of labor before they yield any return whatever in the way of finished products; but when they begin to yield a return, the return is very large. If in the meantime circumstances have changed so that the product is no longer required, the elaborate work of preparation is wasted. Consider the sort of thing that happened at the beginning of the great depression. Everybody had felt rich and had expected to be able to buy all sorts of expensive things. Preparations were made for producing all these expensive things, and then it turned out that the preparations had been excessive. The men who had made preparations for one sort of commodity could not sell their products, and therefore could not buy another sort of commodity, and so the makers of the other sort of commodity could not buy yet a third sort, and so the depression spread. Vast amounts of preparation for the production of commodities suddenly became useless. The men who should have been at work were unemployed, and in their turn could spend much less than had been expected. And so what had been expected to be means of producing wealth became suddenly useless, and everybody was poor. In such a situation everybody's apparent private interest is diametrically opposed to the public interest. The banks which have lent money are afraid that their debtors will go bankrupt and therefore call in loans left and right, thereby causing the bankruptcy that they fear. Dread of disaster makes everybody act in the very way that increases the disaster. Psychologically the situation is analogous to that of people trampled to death when there is a panic in a theater caused by a cry of "Fire!" In the situation that existed in the great depression, things could only be set right by causing the idle plant to work again. But everybody felt that to do so was to risk almost certain loss. Within the framework of classical economics there was no solution. Roosevelt saved the situation by bold and heretical action. He spent billions of public money and created a huge public debt, but by so doing he revived production and brought his country out of the depression. Businessmen, who in spite of such a sharp lesson continued to believe in old-fashioned economics, were infinitely shocked, and although Roosevelt saved them from ruin, they continued to curse him and to speak of him as "the madman in the White House." Except for Fabre's investigation of the behavior of insects, I do not know any equally striking example of inability to learn from experience.

The principle which Roosevelt applied in the New Deal is the same principle which is now needed in international affairs. Although it seems paradoxical, it is nevertheless the fact that the way to avoid poverty is to spend. This, of course, does not apply to private individuals, who cannot spend more than they have, but it does apply to Governments, which alone have the privilege of not paying their debts. Americans have a great desire to sell their goods abroad, but they cannot do so unless foreign nations can afford to buy. I do not wish to say anything that may sound ungenerous about Marshall Aid, but I shall only be repeating what its American advocates have urged, when I say that it serves the interests of America as well as those of Europe. I do not mean only, what undoubtedly is true, that it has halted the spread of Communism in Western Europe. I mean that actually America is better off financially owing to spending money on reviving Europe. Truman's Point 4, which was to have revived countries outside Europe by similar methods, has unfortunately not been understood by Congress, and has been very inadequately implemented. It is to be hoped that further experience will lead America to see its wisdom.

I have spoken of the wastefulness of industrial plant lying idle, but the enforced idleness of human beings is even worse. Idle plant and idle human beings are alike useless, but the idle human beings also suffer. The older economic theory was quite unable to deal with the problem of unemployment. Trade-cycles were regarded as a law of nature, and it was thought that there was no method by which men could be kept in work in bad times. I have sometimes suggested to Americans that the great depression was due to mistakes in American economic policy, and they have stared at me as if I had said that the Government was responsible for the San Francisco earthquake. They were quite unable to believe that such phenomena as trade-cycles can be controlled by human action. We now know, however, that they can be so controlled. We owe this knowledge chiefly to Keynes. The broad principle is that Governments must spend and encourage spending when private people feel inclined to save, and must encourage saving or compel it by means of taxation when private people feel inclined to spend. There seems little doubt that if Governments will adopt the methods advocated by Keynes, there is no reason why trade-cycles should continue, or why there should be periods of large-scale unemployment. Keynes was not a Socialist, but he did advocate Government action for the prevention of crises and depressions. I do not think it can be reasonably maintained that the good results which his system is capable of producing can be produced except through the action of Governments.

There is a general conclusion to be drawn from modern economic development, and that is that any nation which desires to prosper must seek rather co-operation than competition with other nations. The world is economically unified in a way in which it never was at any earlier period. And even in terms of hard cash, it is seldom profitable nowadays for one nation to ruin another. Nay, more, if another nation is ruined, it is almost always profitable for a nation which can afford it to help the ruined nation on the road to recovery. This is because, broadly speaking, nations are more important to each other as customers than as competitors, and also because unemployment is a waste of which the disadvantages are felt, not only in the nation in which the unemployment exists, but in varying degrees throughout the world. Although Congress finds this a little hard to understand, many people in international organizations now realize this. A start in the direction of a world where economic co-operation replaces competition has already been made, not only in the Marshall Plan and the Organization for European Economic Co-operation, but also in the Colombo Plan. Many United Nations agencies, such as the Food and Agriculture Organization, are interested in this problem of increasing the purchasing power of poorer nations, so that the customers of prosperous nations may be increased, and so that both the prosperous and the poorer nations may be more prosperous as a result of this exchange.

This doctrine, which is promulgated by hard-headed economists for hard-headed reasons, encounters obstacles that are psychologically derived from the fetish of competition, and inherited with far too little change from our savage ancestors who knocked each other on the head with clubs.

I have no doubt that the world would now be richer if people were actuated in their economic relations with other nations by altruism and a disinterested desire to avert suffering. Such a feeling would, I am convinced, do more to promote actions in harmony with rational self-interest than is done by the way of feeling which regards foreign nations as rivals and potential enemies. Hatred, I suppose, must be pleasant, since so many people indulge in it; but unlike virtue it is its own reward, and those who choose it must be willing to pay the price.

The Next Half-Century

T HE twentieth century so far has not been a credit to the human race. True, a number of emperors have disappeared, which from the point of view of 1793 would be adjudged a gain. But the results have not always been happy. There are those who may doubt whether Stalin is much better for the world than Nicholas II, whether Hitler was a great improvement on Kaiser Wilhelm, and even (greatly daring) whether Hirohito was much worse than MacArthur. In any case, these transfers were somewhat expensive. Each of them cost many millions of human lives, many billions of dollars, much abasement of the currency of civilization. There were also special horrors, such as the extermination of Jews, the deliberate starvation of Russian peasants, and the invention of the terror of atomic death. These, so far, are the achievements of the twentieth century. There is a risk, a very imminent risk, that, glorious as these achievements are, they will sink into insignificance beside those of the next few years. As I write, I do not know—no one knows—whether London and New York will still exist six months hence. I do not know—no one else of my age in Western Europe knows—whether the children and the grandchildren upon whom care has been lavished will survive another twelve months. I do not know, and no one else knows, what, if anything, will be left of the structure of Western civilization which has been slowly built up from the time of Homer. All this is in doubt. All this depends upon the degree of hysteria in the United States, on the courage of Truman, the independence of Western Europe, and the good or bad temper of the Politburo. I will not venture to prophesy; I will consider only what, if the immediate crisis can be successfully passed, can and should be done to make the future less precarious.

The first and most important thing concerning which I shall have much to say in the remainder of this book, is a change of outlook on the part of Western statesmen and the Western public. We have allowed ourselves to be hypnotized by fear. When I say "fear," I do not mean a rational apprehension of danger. Undoubtedly there is danger; undoubtedly the danger is imminent and terrible. But dangers are not averted by terror; they are averted by calm thought. A captain who finds his ship in danger of sinking is expected to avoid hysteria, but an American statesman in the same situation is thought to be a fellow-traveler if he remains calm.

What the present situation demands is evident. It demands first and foremost sufficient armaments to make Western Europe secure. When this has been achieved, Western Germany and France and Italy will revive spiritually, since they will no longer live under the imminent threat of obliteration. And when the West feels secure against invasion, there will no longer be any risk of a Third World War, unless from the truculence of America. If America can be induced to be less truculent, the whole world will be able to breathe freely once more. When there is security, there will no longer be need for a hostile demeanor in dealings with the Russians. They will in time perceive that the hope of world dominion is vain, and that the best they can expect is to hold their present territories. It will then become necessary to persuade them that we do not wish or intend to conquer them. They are full of suspicion, a suspicion for which it must be said they have grounds, both in the allied intervention at the end of the First World War, and in the present attitude of the most vocal section of American opinion. It will take time to overcome this suspicion, but when once the West has obviously superior strength, and yet does not go to war, it will become year by year easier to make Russia believe that conquest forms no part of our purposes. I believe that when once they are persuaded of this, the harshness of their regime will rapidly grow less, and by slow stages friendly co-operation will become possible. This is not a dramatic policy, but in fact drama is dangerous and should be carefully avoided. If and when Russia becomes less illiberal, international control of atomic energy will become possible, and one of the horrors that darken our imaginations and fill our sleep with nightmares will be dissipated. Then at last the way will be open for the creation of a world Government by agreement. I see no reason why this should not be achieved before the end of the present century.

Meanwhile there are problems in Asia and problems in Africa which, unless wise statesmanship is used, will become daily more threatening and more insoluble. Even if no motive were involved except self-preservation, it would be urgently necessary for the West to find ways of raising Asia and Africa to the economic level of Western Europe, if not of America. So long as this is not done, Asia and Africa will inevitably feel envy, and the envy will turn to destructiveness. While destructive passions dominate half the human race, the other half cannot be safe. Europe and America therefore, even if very considerable immediate sacrifices are involved, will, if they are wise, devote themselves to the economic welfare of populations that are not white. For the reasons that I have given in the last chapter, even a very considerable expenditure in this direction will bring an actual cash reward to the nations that make it, because prosperity in one place tends to produce prosperity in another, and conversely, poverty in one place tends to impoverish another.

For the reasons which I have given in earlier chapters, it will not be enough to invest capital in Asia and Africa, to modernize their agriculture and develop their industry. These things must be done, but whatever improvement they may produce will be very short-lived unless the populations concerned learn to practice the limitation of population. It is common in the West to suppose that there are insuperable psychological and theological obstacles to limitation of population in countries that are now backward. This is an entire mistake. Anyone who will look back to the pronouncement by Nehru which I quoted in an earlier chapter will see that so far as this matter is concerned there is less superstition in the East than in Massachusetts or Connecticut. I do not think any reasonable person can doubt that in India, China and Japan, if the knowledge of birth-control existed, the birth-rate would fall very rapidly. In Africa the process might take longer, but there also it could be fairly easily achieved if Negro doctors, trained in the West, were given the funds to establish medical clinics in which every kind of medical information would be given. I do not suppose that America would contribute to this beneficent work, because if either party favored it, that party would lose the Catholic vote in New York State, and therefore the Presidency. This obviously would be a greater disaster than the extermination of the human race by atomic war. But we need not think that surplus funds will always continue to come only from America. The British and the French have much larger interests in Africa than the Americans have, and given economic recovery, the British and the French will be able to carry out policies in that continent even if America does not actively favor them.

In all suggestions for work by white men in either Asia or

Africa, we are met by the difficulty that past history has made white imperialism suspect. For some reason—certainly a very bad one—Asia and Africa do not regard the Russians as imperialists, even when they see a great country like China reduced to the position of a satellite. But when the Americans, the French or the British attempt any work, however beneficial and however humanitarian, in either Asia or Africa, they are at once suspected of territorial designs. It will take time and patience and honesty to overcome this suspicion; but if European influence were withdrawn suddenly, the result might easily be anarchy and chaos. The problem of preserving European influence where it is fruitful but not where it is imperialistic is a very delicate one. I do not think it can be solved except by people imbued with something like a missionary spirit, not in favor of any Church, but of a rational and productive way of life. There will need to be a large body of men in the West who understand, as few men now understand, what it is that the West has to offer, in its ways of life, its conquest of poverty, its high standard of education and its diminution of disease. These are things depending upon a certain technique. That technique, since it has been a white man's technique, has been intimately associated with white man's imperialism. I met once a Mexican Marxist and I asked him what he considered the message of Marx to Mexico. The message was, he said, that the Maya civilization was superior to that of Spain. This, of course, was because the descendants of the Maya are poor and the descendants of the Spaniards tend to be rich. I do not wish to say a word against Maya civilization, since I know very little about it; still less do I wish to say anything in favor of the civilization of Spain. Nevertheless, in a country full of oil and next door to the United States, I do not think a return to pre-Columbian civilization is a very practical policy. The same kind of problem will arise in other parts of the world. It will be very regrettable if the cessation of Western imperialism prevents the spread of what is good in Western ways of life. If this is to be prevented it will only be by a very considerable expenditure of disinterested zeal on the part of Western technicians and men of science and those who support them.

One of the great dangers of our time is nationalist and theological fanaticism. When one observes that the high idealism of the Indian Government in international matters breaks down completely when confronted with the question of Kashmir, it is difficult to avoid a feeling of despair. Quarrels of Jews and Arabs produce similar emotions, especially when one observes that whichever side is not favored by the State Department feels inclined to call in the Communists, in spite of the steam-roller characteristics of their regime. Another example of the same sort of thing is Ireland. I will not take sides on the Ulster question; I will only observe that both sides apparently consider it more important than the preservation of Western civilization, or even of the human race, a view which to my mind is slightly exaggerated. Then there are premature aspirations. Iran wishes to be independent and has every right to be so, but until the conflict between Russia and the West has been decided, neither party is likely to concede independence to Iran, and certainly Iran is not in a position to exact it at present. There is need everywhere of a much greater knowledge of international affairs and of the place of one's own country in relation to the whole. Until this kind of knowledge is widely disseminated, many fragments will aim at a degree of isolation which is no longer possible. For good or ill, the human race has become one family. It can bring itself to disaster in a family quarrel or to happiness by means of harmony, but no member of the family can effectively cut itself off from the rest—not even Tibet or Chicago, the last refuges of isolationism.

This brings me to the subject of education. If there is to be effective international co-operation, such as was hoped for by the creators of the League of Nations and the United Nations, there will have to be very widespread education of an internationalist character. Schools will have to teach not only the narrow and biased nationalistic history which has hitherto been often thought sufficient, but world history from an impartial point of view. The books to be used in teaching world history will have to be books free from national bias, as far as this is humanly possible. There would have to be devices to secure impartiality. I should have the parts dealing with South America written by Norwegians, but the parts dealing with the Vikings should be written by Italians, and the parts dealing with medieval Italy by Americans. I should try to get all the books of history that would be used in schools written by men imbued with a feeling for man as man, and for human progress as opposed to the progress of this or that particular nation. And a great deal more should be taught about the world of the present day. It is all very well to know about Marathon, but it is not much help in dealing with the troubles of the Anglo-Iranian Oil Company, whose employees should not regard themselves as descendants of the army of Miltiades. Children should from an early age be made aware of the modern interdependence of different groups of men, and the importance of co-operation and the folly of conflict. They should have a new morality of growth and mutual adaptation, with consequent possibilities of freedom, in place of the older morality of prohibitions, conflicts, victories and defeats. In a word, they should be brought up to be citizens of the world in which they will have to live, not of the world of those bygone centuries among which academic culture loves to dwell. I do not mean that they should be ignorant of the past, but I do mean that they should know that it is past, and that our world has need of different beliefs, different desires and different aptitudes from those that were required in technically simpler ages.

No teacher should be tolerated who teaches hostility to some group, whether Jews or Negroes or plutocrats. For it is not by hostility that good things are achieved. I believe myself that the existence of plutocrats is regrettable, but I think the heat and fury generated by a class war is even more regrettable. There is almost always a way, though sometimes a much slower way, of doing things without violence. The French Revolution and the Russian Revolution, in spite of rivers of blood, did not achieve nearly so much towards economic equality as has been achieved in Britain in recent years, without any violence whatever. The teaching of hatred, however socially harmful may be the class against which the hatred is directed, always injects poison into the social system. When the immediate purpose of the hatred has been achieved, the emotion survives as a habit and looks for new victims. All advocacy of social change should be positive and not negative. It should emphasize the good things in a possible future more than the bad things in the present. I do not mean this as an absolute principle. When, for example, it is found that many lunatic asylums practice atrocious cruelties on the patients, it is necessary to concentrate in the first place upon the evil to be abolished. But this is not enough, and if it is thought to be enough, the evil will soon reappear, perhaps in a new form. It is necessary to probe deeper, to discover the causes of the evil, and the sources of malevolence in those who ill-treat their victims. In all such cases there will be found to be some distortion, some impediment to growth, something causing a deep inner discord in those who take pleasure in cruelty. And no reformer should be satisfied until he has arrived at the sources of these psychological misfortunes, and has discovered how to create for the young a world in which such things will not occur. This is a vast task, but it is not beyond the possibilities of economics and psychology combined. The world could within a couple of generations be made to consist of men and women who would be happy and sane, and because they were happy and sane, would be kindly in their impulses towards others, since they would have no impulse to regard others as their enemies in the absence of positive evidence. What we know about the formation of character is, as yet, very insufficiently utilized knowledge. It must be utilized to the full if we are to create a world where men are more prone to like each other than to feel mutual hatred. But of all this I shall speak more fully in the next part.

I have spoken in this chapter on the assumption that a third world war will be avoided, but this is a very doubtful assumption. Any day a third world war may be upon us. If it happens, it will be far more terrible than the two that have preceded it, and will postpone for an indefinite period of time the realization of such hopes as I am dealing with in this book. But it will not postpone them for ever. Those among us who wish to see the sort of world that men could now create must not lose faith and hope if a third world war descends upon them. It will not be the end of the world; it will be a long illness, but not death, and it will be our duty, through whatever darkness and whatever sorrow, to keep hope alive and to bend our thoughts, in spite of present misery, upon the future of which that misery is perhaps only the labor pangs. Men are slow to learn, even when all that is to be learned is the road to happiness. Perhaps they can only learn by even more bitter experience than they have already had of the opposite road. But if they are to learn, if torture is to bring them sanity rather than madness, it will only be because some men have preserved sanity and hope throughout. And the more such men there are, the more chance there is that experience will bring wisdom. Each separate one of us can do something to increase this chance, by steadfastness and courage throughout the days of darkness.

PART III

Man and Himself

XVI

Ideas Which Have Become
Obsolete

HUMAN beings, ever since their fathers invented language, have allowed themselves to be dominated by tradition. This has been at once the main cause of progress and the main obstacle to progress. Consider it first as a cause of progress. Where should we be if each generation had to invent reading, writing and arithmetic for itself? How should we get on if arts and crafts were not handed on? Even in the most progressive age, much the greater part of our activity is, and must be, based upon tradition. We may rebel against our parents' narrow-mindedness, but we can only rise above them by standing on their shoulders.

But although respect for tradition and obedience to custom are necessary up to a point, most societies have carried them much too far, and some have brought themselves to destruction by this sole defect. Human beings change their ways much more quickly than animals do; civilized men change their ways more quickly than uncivilized men, and modern civilized men change their ways more quickly than civilized men of former ages. Civilized societies during the last hundred and fifty years have radically transformed their physical environment, the methods by which they secure a livelihood, and the apparatus of comfort over and above the minimum necessary for survival. The prime cause of these changes has been a vast increase of knowledge and skill.

The new techniques in the material realm demand, if they are to bring their full benefit in increase of human welfare, an accompaniment of new mental habits. It is in this respect more than in any other that our world falls short. In an age of machines and skilled scientific production, we retain the feelings and many of the beliefs that were appropriate to the ages of scarcity and primitive agriculture. Political ideas are almost exactly what they were in the eighteenth century. In the eighteenth century they worked, after a fashion; now they are heading straight to disaster. Let no Communist imagine that his creed is exempt from this charge; on the contrary, their political ideas are peculiarly old-fashioned, being exactly like those of Philip II in the sixteenth century or Louis XIV in the seventeenth. But although Communists are in this respect the most reactionary, the rest of us also, though in a lesser degree, have need of new ways of thinking and feeling.

The need of new political and social ideas is due to our increase of efficiency, both for good and evil. In the old days many things that are now possible could not be achieved by any known means. Extreme poverty for the great majority was unavoidable. Population perpetually pressed upon the limits of subsistence, except when it was catastrophically diminished by famine or pestilence. Wars created aristocracies of conquerors, who lived without compunction upon the labor of the vanquished. It was not until the French Revolution that this system began to be superseded by one involving less general misery. Now, in certain important Western countries extreme poverty has almost disappeared, famine is unknown, large-scale pestilences have yielded to medical science, and a low birth-rate has made it possible to preserve a high level of prosperity when it has been reached. All this is new in human history. Struggle, fight, starvation and premature death have been the lot of the great majority of human beings ever since there were human beings, just as they were the lot of the animals before them.

The fundamental source of this beneficent revolution is scientific production, and the scientific habit of mind which has given rise to it. Two other things besides scientific methods of production have been necessary, namely democracy and a low birth-rate, but these by themselves would not have been sufficient, and would scarcely have been possible without science except for brief periods in exceptional circumstances. Though not sufficient to produce a happy community, they are necessary, and machine industry without them may lead to a new form of serfdom quite as dreadful as anything in the gloomy annals of the past.

We hear much about the Western way of life and the need of defending it against the Eastern menace. But few in the West are clear as to the essentials of the Western way of life, or as to what makes it worth defending. If we were clear about this our propaganda would be more effective, and we should have less need than we have at present to depend upon military might as our sole protection.

What the West has discovered (though as yet the realization is incomplete) is a method by which practically everybody can have as much of material goods as is conducive to happiness, without excessive hours of labor, and with that degree of mental culture that is needed to make leisure delightful. This is rendered possible by the fact that one man's work can now produce much more than is required for one man's subsistence. But as yet this system has only a precarious life. It is threatened from without by those whom envy renders destructive, and it is threatened from within by those who are still under the domination of beliefs and passions appropriate to a bygone age.

The kernel of these beliefs and passions is the STRUGGLE FOR LIFE. Where this struggle is now still necessary, it is necessary because men are misguided, not because nature is niggardly. In former times, if two men each wished to live on the produce of a piece of land which only yielded enough for one, they must either both starve or fight till one was killed. In practice, it was not single men who fought, but groups of men, called successively tribes, nations, coalitions, or United Nations. In spite of Christianity, which enjoined peace before the necessary industrial technique had been invented, sheer necessity drove men into conflict. As it was the victors who left descendants, it was the mentality of victors that was handed down. The vanquished may, in dying, have repented of their temerity, but their repentance came too late to save their children, and what the next generation imbibed from their parents was the righteousness of timely aggression. And so war came to be surrounded with a halo of virtue. On Sundays men pretended to believe that the meek shall inherit the earth, but on weekdays they effectively believed the exact opposite. The Christian virtues, up to a point, could be tolerated within the tribe, but in dealings with those outside it what was prized was courage, ruthlessness and ferocity disguised under the name of patriotism.

Nor was it only in external relations that the ethic of struggle was operative. In a community in which a few lived in luxury while the great majority were on the verge of destitution, it was inevitable that those who acquired luxury and power should inculcate beliefs and feelings which caused them to be admired. Where the possession of land was the chief source of wealth, as it was almost everywhere before the coming of industrialism, the qualities likely to be found among landowners came to be thought ethically admirable. In this respect, the history of words is interesting. A "chivalrous" man meant, originally, a man who owned a horse. A "noble" man was a man who had an ancestor sufficiently powerful to possess a coat of arms. Generally the people who were most looked up to were those who, by devious or ruthless means, had acquired exceptional power. In such a society the effective morality, however disguised by fine phrases, was inevitably one of a struggle to the death.

The coming of industrialism, though it altered the form of the struggle for existence, did not alter the substance of it or the moral ideas associated with it. There were, it is true, certain important changes: wealth was less derived from land, and was less often hereditary. But this only intensified the struggle, since it diminished the security of the successful. Industrialism at first, while it enormously increased the wealth of the rich, made the poor even poorer than before. And in countries accustomed to aristocracy it was difficult to transfer to the new rich the awed respect which had been bestowed through centuries upon "blue blood." But although admiration for the new rich had its limits, it was easy to generate a superstitious admiration for the system that made them rich, and competition was erected into a kind of god. And so industrialism, which is technically capable of bringing peace to mankind, in fact brought not peace but a sword.

Competition, as conceived by its early devotees, was to be kept within bounds. It was to be confined to rival employers, and limited to what the law allowed. But it escaped from these shackles. There was competition between classes, and there was competition between nations. The first led to Socialism, the second to war. Neither of these had been intended by the early apostles of competition, such as Cobden, and yet both were inevitable consequences of the creed. Both, in their modern form, result from the unwillingness of the less fortunate to acquiesce tamely in an inferior status, combined with the unwillingness of the more fortunate to tolerate any approach to equality unless it can be extorted by force. This unwillingness of the more fortunate is due to their failure to apprehend the possibilities of the new age of plenty, or the disasters to be feared from technically efficient strife. As industrialism becomes more and more efficient, the old competitive outlook becomes at once less applicable and more harmful, since both plenty and disastrous devastation are possible results of human skill.

I wish to repeat that the whole basis of the change of outlook which is required is technical. There is nowadays much more profit in large-scale co-operation than there used to be. The food of industrial regions comes from overseas; so as a rule do many of the raw materials. Vast unifications are profitable, whereas dislocations caused by wars or strikes do more harm than they did in former times. With modern technique, given an adequate political organization, everybody throughout the world could enjoy material comfort; but the habit of rivalry is so engrained owing to the millennia during which it was profitable that most people are still convinced that what makes others poor must make them rich. Before the First World War, the British were terrified of German competition, and the Germans equally believed that it would be to their advantage to ruin England. It was the Germans who were ruined, but what English industrialist would pretend that the British were the richer for the war? Although the Germans were ruined, the British were impoverished; both would have been much richer if they could have made a business deal and co-operated as a single unit.

Just the same considerations apply to the present East-West tension. The Russians believe, whether sincerely or not, that they can only prosper by first ruining the West. The West not unnaturally concludes that it can only survive by first ruining Russia. I will not for a moment deny that while these reciprocal sentiments exist, they make themselves true. If A and B each know that the other is after him with a pistol, they may consider general maxims about the desirability of co-operation irrelevant. The question for each reduces itself to the very simple one, "which of us will kill the other first." But the difference between their interests is caused by their sentiments, not by any external natural cause, and so it is with the public enmities in the modern world. They have no justification in economic fact or sober self-interest, but result solely from the surviving pugnacity of mankind, which once served a purpose but now is merely antiquated.

The division of the world into nations has two aspects, one cultural and one political. I see no reason to regret the cultural division. Different nations have different kinds of merits, and it is not to be wished that all the world should be alike, but there is no reason why cultural diversity should imply political enmity. For 750 years the English and the French fought each other under the impression that their interests conflicted. At last they discovered that this had been a mistake, and since 1815 they have been good friends. There is no reason but the tyranny of ancient habit why this should not happen in other cases. Take again the case of Russia and the West. If each became convinced that the other had no hostile intentions, each would be spared all the expense of armaments, each would derive benefits from reciprocal commerce, each would escape from the dread of the atomic bomb and the destruction of large parts of the population. The motives of self-interest which on each side promote hostile feeling are merely a reflection of the exactly identical motives of self-interest of the other side, and are based on each side upon the assumption that the other side is irrationally inclined. Of course human nature being what it is, this naked analysis will seem shocking to both sides, for wherever hostility exists, however obsolete may be its sources, it appears on both sides as a great moral crusade, in which it is the duty of every true man to uphold high ethical ideals. But all this is merely a part of the psychological camouflage by which *homo sapiens* conceals from himself his own lack of wisdom. Suppose some drug were discovered which removed mental mists from the mind, and suppose that the only two people who had taken this drug were Stalin and Mr. Truman, what do you think would happen? Presumably they would meet in a neutral spot, they would shake hands and share a drink, and each would say to the other: "Well, old boy, I suppose you are really not much worse than I am." They would then in the course of half an hour at most find an equitable solution of all the problems in which the interests of their respective nations were popularly supposed to be conflicting. They would go home jubilant; but Stalin would be assassinated by Molotov, and Mr. Truman would be successfully impeached by Senator McCarthy. After this each nation would return to its former folly.

What I wish to illustrate by this pleasant fairy tale is that we cannot blame Governments for our troubles, nor can they be cured by merely governmental action. What is needed is a change in the ordinary outlook of ordinary people. The change that is wanted is sometimes thought to be a moral change, but my own belief is that nothing is required beyond a just estimate of self-interest. I know that it is difficult to rouse enthusiasm for such a view. Suppose you said to a population: "If you pursue course A, half of you will die in agony and the other half will live in squalor; whereas if you pursue course B you will all prosper." And suppose that on this basis you conducted a great political campaign. What do you think would happen? All the earnest moralists would rise up and say: "Sir, your aims are base. There are more important things than material prosperity. Should a great nation shrink from suffering if it is incurred in a noble cause? Was it by such degraded self-seeking that our ancestors made our nation great? Perish the thought! Away with money grubbers. Let us live like heroes, and if fate so wills it, die like heroes." You will find that you are completely powerless against the mass hysteria so generated. You will find men pointing the finger of scorn at you as a coward, and you will be lucky if your "cowardice" does not lead to your being lynched, while the thousands who are lynching you contrast their inflexible courage with your base poltroonery.

I do not wish to draw a pessimistic conclusion from what I have just been saying. There is a kind of wiseacre who will tell you with a portentous air that you will never succeed in changing human nature, and that human nature loves fighting. "You will never manage to put an end to war," he says with pretended sorrow but real glee. You may reply: "My dear Sir, I think you are displaying some ignorance of the modern art of war. Do you not know that unless an end is put to war by agreement within the next fifty years, an end will be put to war by another and even more efficient method, namely the extermination of the human race?" At that the wiseacre will only splutter.

The dictum that human nature cannot be changed is one of those tiresome platitudes that conceal from the ignorant the depths of their own ignorance. None of those who utter this platitude know anything about the investigations of psychologists into what is congenital and what is acquired in the character of an adult. Those who are experimenting on newborn babies tell us that they have three instincts apart from that of feeding. They are frightened if they find themselves without support; they are angered if the movement of their limbs are constricted; and they are pleased if they are skillfully tickled. This apparently is the sum total of their repertoire. It is easy to see how political slogans develop out of this material, but it is also easy to see that what the slogans will be is quite different in one environment from what they will be in another. Students of anthropology know that what happens in some cultures seems to people brought up in other cultures totally contrary to what they imagine to be human nature. When it is said that the love of fighting is a part of human nature, there are two things that may be meant. On the one hand, anybody may be made angry by certain kinds of provocation: few men are so saintly as to display no annoyance if someone pulls their nose. On the other hand, there are in some people impulses of aggression and a positive pleasure in combat. It is only these people that constitute a problem, since the other people can be placated by the simple technique of not pulling their noses. That there is in many men at present this impulse of aggression I will not deny. But it is an impulse generated in the course of their upbringing, and by no means an inevitable part of the make-up of adult character. Consider the example of dueling: when dueling was a recognized practice, it was argued that every gentleman must resent an insult, and it was implied that every gentleman might inflict an insult if he were willing to fight the ensuing duel. The result of this was that people whose manners were supposed to be perfect could behave abominably to other people, and that other people were branded as cowards if they were not willing to show their resentment by dying for a punctilio. Since dueling has gone out of fashion, a man who insults another is considered to be an ill-mannered fellow, and incurs the contempt of the community. Thus the abolition of a recognized method of resenting insults has caused insults to go out of fashion. This illustrates the kind of change that is needed if the world is to adapt itself to modern conditions.

There is still in some countries a quite irrational and unjustifiable admiration of he-men, and this admiration affects the education of boys from the age of four upwards. The boy is admired if he is "tough," that is to say if he is prepared at any moment to enforce his own wishes upon boys who are less ready or less efficient with their fists. To be amenable to arguments of justice where one's own interests are involved is thought to be a sign of weakness. The boy who has been admired by his parents, his teachers and his sisters for the brutality of his behavior grows up into a bully. He finds pleasure in getting the better of his own class by unfair competition, and at the same time he likes to see his own class combined against the rest of the nation, to perpetuate the possession of privileges. In international dealings he has a contempt for aliens, whom he considers to be sniveling and devious. He would rather bludgeon them into agreements they detest than conclude on equal terms agreements advantageous to both parties.

Correlative to the he-man is the she-woman, who is equally undesirable. She likes brutality in males, and feels that she is securing safety in a dangerous world when she marries a man who is always prepared to knock people down on the slightest provocation. She is not afraid of her husband's brutality because she knows he is stupid, and she is persuaded that she can always get the better of him by feminine wiles. Every display of insensate pugnacity on his part provides her with an opportunity of flattery. So the more they love each other, the worse they both become.

It is not to be supposed that such characters benefit their own community, under modern conditions. In the past Genghis Khan and Tamerlain secured wealth and luxury for their own followers by the simple process of exterminating the inhabitants of conquered countries. The Russians have adopted a somewhat similar plan in East Prussia but now it is less advantageous than more humane methods would be. One of the most vexing things for the modern he-man is the complexity of our civilization, which makes it impossible to know what will be advantageous unless you are prepared to exert some modicum of intelligence. Intelligence, as every he-man knows, is a contemptible quality. The boys who display much at school are seldom good at games, and can usually be kicked without fear of retaliation, and yet there are many things of obvious importance which only people possessing a certain intelligence can understand. One of these is finance. That is why Andrew Jackson—a typical he-man—could not stand banks. He knew how to kill men in a duel, but he did not know how to get the better of a bank manager. So, in 1920, the he-men took control of American finance, and by 1932 they had brought America and the rest of the world to the brink of ruin. Nevertheless, they continued to resent the policy by which further ruin was averted, because it could only be understood by more intelligence than they chose to exert. Hatred of intelligence is one of the great dangers of the modern world, because with each new advance in technique intelligence becomes more necessary. I have spoken of finance, but intelligence is equally necessary in everything else. Progress in industrial technique depends upon inventors. Progress in war depends upon atomic physicists, not one of whom would have won the respect of his "manly" contemporaries. Wisdom in international affairs requires knowledge of geography, an acquaintance with the habits of various nations, and a capacity for seeing how the world looks from a point of view that is not your own, none of which can be obtained without intelligence. Our great democracies still tend to think that a stupid man is more likely to be honest than a clever man, and our politicians take advantage of this prejudice by pretending to be even more stupid than nature made them.

This popular fear of intelligence is one of the great dangers of our times, and like the other prejudices of which I have been speaking, it is a matter primarily for the schools. If teachers and educational authorities had more understanding of the sort of person the modern world needs, they could within a generation produce an outlook that would transform the world. But their ideal of character is an old-fashioned one.

They admire most the sort of character which would give a man leadership in a gang of pirates, and if you say that commerce is a different thing from piracy, they think you soft and hope you are mistaken. All this is due to the persistence of old martial ideas that have descended to us from earlier ages. These ideas, I repeat, were appropriate to an age of unavoidable scarcity, but are not applicable to our own times, when whatever scarcity still exists is due to human stupidity and to nothing else. Although this is the case, most of us still prefer passion to intelligence, we like to have our feelings roused, we like to cheer and boo, we like to admire and we like to hate, we like to see things in black and white. Our whole mental apparatus is that which is appropriate to sending us rushing into battle with hoarse war-cries.

Consider the application of such a mentality to international banking, and you will not be surprised by the great depression which it produced whilst it reigned unchecked, nor by the belief of the Nazis that the depression could be curbed if only enough Jews were exterminated, nor by the Russian belief that we should all be rich if all the rich men were liquidated. None of these mistakes would have been made by men in whom intelligence was capable of controlling passion, none of them would have been made by men who understood that when different groups have different interests it is because of unwise passions and not because of any physical fact.

The world is facing a prospective disaster, and is asking itself in a bewildered way why there seems no escape from a tragic fate that no one desires. The fundamental reason is that we have not adapted our mentality to our technique. We still allow ourselves ways of thinking and feeling that were appropriate in a technically simpler age. If we are to live happily with a modern technique—and it is possible for modern technique to bring a far higher level of happiness than was formerly possible—we must banish certain ideas and substitute certain others. For love of domination we must substitute equality; for love of victory we must substitute justice; for brutality we must substitute intelligence; for competition we must substitute co-operation. We must learn to think of the human race as one family, and further our common interests by the intelligent use of natural resources, marching together towards prosperity, not separately towards death and destruction. The mental change required is difficult, and will not be achieved in a moment, but if the need is recognized by educators, and if the young are brought up as citizens of this world and not of a bygone world of predatory warriors, the change can be achieved within a generation, so that we may hope to save at least a portion of mankind from the universal destruction with which we are threatened by the pursuit of obsolete ideas.

XVII

Fear

THE greatest obstacle to a good world is now FEAR. This was not always the case. The life of primitive man could not have been other than difficult and painful—in the classical phrase, "nasty, brutish, and short." And until our own day the great majority of mankind had to toil more than was compatible with a happy and free development. This is still the case in large parts of the world, but it need not be. We now know what is necessary if man is to escape from these ancient evils. The ancient evils were reflected within in the form of fears. To a large extent these fears corresponded to real external dangers, but as far back as we can study man, there were also superstitious fears that expressed merely the tyranny of the habit of fear, extended beyond what the circumstances demanded. In the modern world, the excess of fear above the level which may be called rational is more marked than ever before, because the habit of fear persists while the occasions for fear have greatly diminished.

The human mind is a microcosm, not of the world as it is but of the world as it was. The human mind is in layers, like geological strata. The feelings to which we are prone are those that were appropriate to our ancestors at various stages of their development. The feelings that lie deepest, that belong to those unconscious regions that are explored by psychoanalysis, are very largely such as were appropriate to primitive man, or even to his pre-human precursors. Above this lowest layer come feelings appropriate to barbarians, to the earliest civilized men, to the Greco-Roman world, and to those who destroyed it. In the level of conscious thought, advanced thinkers have sometimes got as far as ideas appropriate to the eighteenth century. But conscious thought is not enough. As everyone now knows, it is difficult to exaggerate the extent to which feelings dictate beliefs; and while the feelings remain unconscious their effect in impeding rationality cannot be effectively counteracted. The human mind, like the human body, is a product of two kinds of factors: those that are congenital, and those that are due to environment. In the body, the congenital factors outweigh the environmental ones. You cannot by education or diet turn a man into a hippopotamus. But where the mind is concerned, the environmental factors outweigh those that are congenital. This is not surprising, since the most important congenital factor distinguishing human from animal minds is the capacity of learning by experience, that is to say, of being influenced by environment. A great many features of most minds at the present day, although historically they are connected with conditions of life in very primitive times, are nevertheless produced in each individual by his present-day environment. Certain habits of thought and feeling grew up long ago, and have been transmitted from age to age by the example and instruction of parents. It is important to be clear on this point, because what is environmental can be quickly changed by change in environment and by new methods of education, whereas what is congenital can only be changed by the slow operation of natural selection. This at least is true at present. It may be that science will discover hereafter methods of changing congenital factors, but such possibilities lie still in the rather distant future. For the present it is to the environmental factors that we must look for the possibilities of change and improvement.

Fears are, broadly speaking, of three kinds: there is fear of external nature; there is fear of other men; and there is fear of our own impulses.

Fear of physical nature formed necessarily a very large part of primitive human life. Men could only keep alive by being alert and perpetually on the watch for possible disasters. If you spread crumbs for the birds on your window-sill in frosty weather, you will observe in the birds a vivid conflict between hunger and fear. Gradually the bolder ones make a dash for a crumb and quickly retire. Their example encourages the others, and after a time the birds that live in your neighbor-hood get to know that you are harmless. But even then you will see that while they are picking up crumbs their glances are darting this way and that in perpetual readiness to notice any approaching danger. This is how early man must have felt. And man in our day has only half-learned the lesson that the environment is not as dangerous as he is inclined to suppose.

There are, of course, physical dangers. There are earth-quakes and shipwrecks, and in the valleys of great rivers there are occasional floods which sweep away multitudes of inhabit-ants along with their houses and all their possessions. And there are dangers that are more individual. You may die of thirst in a desert, or of cold in a blizzard; but such things statistically are not very frequent causes of death in modern civilized communities. They still, however, play a disproportionate part in dreams and phantasies. Everybody has had at some time nightmares of falling, which seem to suggest an origin in the lives of our arboreal ancestors, though this perhaps is fanciful. Hymns and myths tend to speak of refuges from storm and of images of water in a parched land. Moses striking the rock makes a universal appeal, even to those who have never been very thirsty. Hymns represent heaven as a refuge from the storms of life, not as a place where one escapes the dangers of being run over by a motor-bus, although the latter danger is a much more frequent experience in modern urban life.

We are, in fact, so emotionally conditioned to a life of physical danger, that many people find existence tame without it. Schoolmasters escape from the humdrum condition of their scholastic existence to perilous climbs in the Alps. So far as the police will allow, young men like to drive cars in a manner endangering the lives not only of others but of themselves. A certain element of risk exists in many of the pleasures that people seek in their spare time. This illustrates a general rule which is one of the causes of difficulty in a modern world. This rule is that people have emotional needs belonging to an earlier kind of life, and are no longer satisfied in a natural manner by the way of life that they have to adopt. The man who has to take a train to the City every morning and return at the rush hour in the evening has an emotional nature adapted to hunting deer through the forests. If he is sufficiently successful in business he finally rents a deer forest in the Highlands, and at last lives as nature prompted him to live throughout the dreary years in the City. And so, if people are to feel emotionally fulfilled in modern life, they must be allowed a modicum of danger from time to time. If possible it ought to be danger only to themselves, as in Alpine climbing. When the danger takes the form of war it becomes a little too serious, and has effects outside the circle of those who are seeking enjoyable risks. If a society is to be stable in spite of eliminating risk from daily life it will have to supply opportunities of holiday risks for those who cannot bear a wholly secure existence.

I come now to fear of other men, which is socially much more important than fear of nature. Fear of other men is, in a sense, completely rational. Most men have in their nature a certain amount of malevolence, and are not reluctant to do a bad turn to another man if they can do so with safety. For the

moment I am not thinking of group hostilities, such as enmities between nations and classes and creeds. I am thinking
for the moment of private malevolence, the sort that exists
proverbially between rivals in the same office, and between
mothers-in-law and daughters-in-law. Rivalry is very deeply
imbedded in human nature as we know it, though not, I believe, in human nature as it might become. Mrs. Brown wishes
to have a better car than Mrs. Jones. And among the men in
an office who are grand enough to have private rooms, there
may be an elaborate competition as to who shall have the best
room. This form of rivalry is especially prominent in America,
where there is little else to mark social superiority. A man has
to exchange his car for a new one long before it is worn out,
since otherwise his wife will be ashamed to show her face
before his neighbors' wives. You can read about this in any
bad American novel.

With rivalry goes envy. At a gathering of eminent authors,
the uninitiated might suppose that there would be brilliant
conversation on interesting literary topics, but this, alas, would
be an illusion. The conversation, in fact, is almost sure to be
a boasting match about royalties. Eminent authors may be
admired by the general public, but by those of somewhat less
eminence they are almost sure to be hated. If any one of them
falls into a scandal which lowers him in the scale, all the smaller
fry will yap with delight. The same sort of thing applies to
politicians. In the year 1910, when I was somewhat younger
than I am now and therefore more naïve, I felt very strongly
the importance of a victory for the Liberals in the contest
about the Budget and the House of Lords. The chief pro-
tagonists in the first election of 1910 were Lloyd George and
Winston Churchill. I admired both for their able work on
behalf of the common cause, and I foolishly supposed they
admired each other. But on penetrating a little more intimately
into Liberal political circles, I found, on the contrary, that

there was a bitter rivalry between their followers, and that each group could have derived almost as much pleasure from the other's failure as from its own success.

Rivalry, envy, and competitiveness are all based upon insecurity, and therefore upon fear. When a savage tribe is short of food, the last to suffer from the shortage is the chief. It is therefore a good thing to be a chief. The primitive mentality engendered by this situation survives even in such apparently remote contests as a competition between two men for the premiership. Most people feel more insecure than in fact they are. And the only road to security that they can think of is one that enables them to climb on the shoulders of other people.

It is fear that produces social conformity. I knew a very eminent man who rose to world-wide fame, to office and a peerage, but who, on the first occasion when I had a meal in his presence, carefully glanced round the table to see which was the proper implement at this stage. Somewhere deep down in his unconscious was a feeling that the pack might set upon him if he did not show himself to be a completely correct member of the herd. Undoubtedly eminence would diminish this fear, but when I first knew him he was not yet eminent. Boys at school are apt to endure considerable physical and mental suffering if other boys consider them odd. This means that most boys of unusual intelligence have to learn elaborate methods of concealment which are apt to cling to them through later life. They have to pretend to be more "tough" and less intelligent than in fact they are. They have to learn to conceal any enjoyment they may derive from poetry or music. Above all they have to hide as deeply as they possibly can any powers of imagination that they may possess. If they learn to do all this successfully they may slip through without much outward suffering until they become old enough to go to the university. But by this time many of them will have acquired an armor so thick that the living being underneath can hardly peep out.

Social conformity is just as important in the lives of women, though with them it takes slightly different forms. Well-to-do American women all have the same books lying on their table, read the same reviews of the books, and pick out the same remarks in the reviews as expressive of their own opinions. To be a Democrat in the North or a Republican in the South requires a degree of courage which is very rare among those that have good incomes. What is even more important than correct opinions is correct furniture, correct appointments on the dinner-table, correct clothes, and correctly graduated friendliness. Given all these things, a woman can be accepted as no worse than her neighbors. But woe befall her if she should attempt originality of any sort or kind. Her own conventionality, and her neighbors' unfriendliness if she is unconventional, are alike dictated by fear—fear of the hostility of the pack. This fear is very deep in most societies. It impedes originality and promotes persecution; it prevents growth and individuality and all delicacy of adaptation; and it tends to cause societies to become sterile, stereotyped and cruel.

The instinctive fear-reaction is extremely quick and sure. Suppose somebody advances an opinion which, not being that of the majority of your social group, strikes you as subversive, you will feel instantly, if you are not on your guard against such feelings, that an opinion of this sort will let loose the floods of revolution, deprive you of your livelihood, and loosen all the bonds of morality by which society is held together. Suppose, for example, that you live in the Southern United States and that some Negro has been condemned to death for a rape of which he was innocent; if you speak up for him, you will instantly be regarded as subversive, and as one who has no proper horror of his crime. It will be useless to plead that you do not think that he committed the crime; this will be taken as only a further proof that you do not reprobate the crime as you should. There will be raised eyebrows, whispers, and at last a very widespread hostility. It may be that those who act in this hostile manner in their hearts agree with you, but fear will cause them to pretend that they do not. Indeed, their secret agreement may make them more vocal in opposition. Essentially similar conditions arise everywhere.

I come now to another sort of fear, namely, the fear of alien groups. This fear is most prominent in those who have least experience of groups other than their own. Whatever is strange is terrifying so long as it remains strange. If you had never met anybody who was not a Christian, you would be terrified of Mohammedans. If you had never met anybody who was not a Mohammedan, you would be terrified of Christians. If you have never met a Socialist, you will suspect him of having bombs in his pockets or stealing your spoons. If you have never met a free-thinker, you will suppose that free-thinkers are totally indifferent to all the usages of society. And so on.

I will not say that such fears are totally irrational. Practically all societies are held together by beliefs which reason would find it difficult to justify, and persons belonging to a different society threaten such beliefs. The elder Cato, who was a stern believer in the old Roman virtues, was deeply shocked by the skepticism of Greek philosophers, and held that they should go back where they came from. In a sense he was right. Roman society under the solvent influence of Greek culture lost is monolithic homogeneity, and found itself plunged into civil war. Nevertheless, a point of view such as that of the elder Cato makes adaptation to new circumstances impossible, and imposes immovable obstacles against every kind of reform. Life cannot be freed from all danger, and if it were it would become intolerably tedious.

Risks must be run, and those who shiver at the slightest approach of risk will, if they are successful, condemn their society to barrenness and ossification. Moreover, the kind of horror which ultra-conservative people feel when confronted with anything unfamiliar is one of the great causes of wars and persecutions and large-scale cruelties. The Jews are strange and therefore cause fears which are felt to justify pogroms. Negroes are strange, and therefore it is foolishly fussy to object to an occasional lynching. The Japanese were strange, and there was therefore less compunction in using atom bombs against them than there would have been in the case of the Germans. For although we might have disapproved of the Nazis most of us knew many Germans, and were aware that they had two eyes, a nose and a mouth like other people; but as regards the Japanese we were not so sure. The basis of all such hostilities is fear. The way to diminish the operation of fears of this sort is to make people more aware of the common human characteristics of people who at first sight seem very different from ourselves, and also to bring about the realization that in the modern world, conflicts of interest are unnecessary. The first of these things could be accomplished by the cinema, the second by school education.

One of the effects of fear is submission to leaders. Any social group which is feeling acute fear looks instinctively for a leader whom it believes that it can trust. Sometimes the leader is good, sometimes he is bad, but the instinctive mechanism is the same in either case. It was the same impulse that caused the English to look to Churchill in 1940 and that caused the Germans to look to Hitler in the great depression. Submission to leaders in times of danger is often necessary. It is obvious that in a shipwreck it is a good thing for people to obey the captain. But there are certain inevitable evils in submission to leaders which make it regrettable if fear brings about such submission when it is unnecessary. Submission to leaders takes away the sense of individual responsibility and the habit of individual thought. If the chosen leader is not exceptionally high-minded, he will sooner or later betray his followers for the sake of his own interests, as happened almost invariably with Greek tyrants. And since his power is based upon a general diffused fear, he will probably do little to dissipate such fear, but will, on the contrary, encourage belief in threats from enemies. The result will be witch-hunts within, and wars without. This whole tragic sequence is an outcome of the fear that men feel towards their fellow-men.

I come now to fear of self, which in the modern world has become to a very great extent the basis of the other fears. Every man has impulses which cause him to run into danger. At times he becomes uncontrollably angry. He may insult his boss, or be rude to an uncle from whom he has expectations, or even, if he is sufficiently uncontrolled, whip out his revolver and shoot a man in a fit of rage. Law and politeness demand a certain degree of submissiveness which is often difficult, and a man who is aware of his own angers and rebellions tries hard to keep them under. Another set of impulses which people find difficult to fit into the framework of civilized life are the impulses connected with sex, not only sexual attraction, but also jealousy. These two antagonistic impulses, sex attraction and jealousy, are those which it has been found most difficult to subdue within the received code of social morals. And that is why they supply the theme of most novels and plays. When a man falls in love with another man's wife, he risks being shot by the other man, and the other man risks legal punishment for the shooting. The two impulses of attraction and jealousy, therefore, are both dangerous, and if you wish to slip through life safely, you must learn to control them.

There are two kinds of morality, which may be called respectively "fear morality" and "hope morality." Fear morality seeks to avoid disaster, whereas hope morality seeks to create something that is felt to be good or delightful. Fear morality has been very much more prominent in the creation of moral codes, and in the ethical consciousness of individuals. Sin, or guilt, as psychoanalysts prefer to call it, consists essentially in yielding to impulses that are a cause of danger. Fear morality considers it impossible either to prevent the circumstances causing such impulses or to find them harmless outlets. It sets to work to deal with them by increasing the fear which they arouse, and by threatening other misfortunes in addition to those which they naturally entail. You must not indulge your anger, not only because it is in fact risky to do so, but also because there is something called the moral law which condemns anger, and makes indulgence in anger an example of sin. Sometimes, it is true, a moralist confines himself to pointing out the real dangers. As it says in the Gospels: "Agree with thine adversary quickly, whiles thou art in the way with him, lest at any time the adversary deliver thee to the judge, and the judge deliver thee to the officer, and thou be cast into prison. Verily I say unto thee, Thou shalt by no means come out thence, till thou hast paid the uttermost farthing" (Matthew 5: 25, 26). But three verses before this there is a different statement: "Whosoever is angry with his brother without a cause shall be in danger of the judgment: and whosoever shall say unto his brother, Raca, shall be in danger of the council: but whosoever shall say, Thou fool, shall be in danger of hell fire." All this is put as an extension of the prohibition of murder. By bringing in hell fire it increases the fear which would naturally restrain a man from aggression against his neighbor, without supplying any motive other than fear to divert a man from aggressive behavior.

There is, of course, a positive precept, namely: "Thou shalt love thy neighbor as thyself." Now if you do love your neighbor, all is well, but it is impossible to feel anything deserving the name of love merely because the moral law says you should feel it. Our feelings are not to this degree in the control of our will, and a man who is full of aggressive impulses, but accepts Christian teaching, will be guilty of hypocrisy if he pretends that he really loves his neighbor. There are, in fact, two psychologically very different emotions that can be called love of your neighbor: one is the emotion inspired by fear, namely the feeling that it is not safe to behave towards him in a hostile manner for fear of retaliation. This does not deserve the name of love; it is a piece of practical prudence, leaving your aggressive impulses undiminished, even if you successfully restrain them. But there is another emotion which can be felt at times towards certain people; it is that of taking delight in them. You may take delight in a person with whom you are in love; you may take delight in your children, especially if they are beautiful and gay and affectionate. This is something quite different from the sort of love that you can feel because of a moral precept. It is something in which fear plays no part, and it is something which, where it is strong and satisfying, can altogether remove impulses to hostile aggression. When you contemplate a beautiful landscape or a beautiful picture, you do not, if you are sane, have any impulse to destroy it, and you do not say to yourself "I must love this landscape, lest it should rise up and smite me." When you feel in this way towards a human being, it is easy to behave well towards him, without need of self-control and without gloomy apprehensions of hell fire if you should call him a fool. This kind of emotion, whenever it is possible, is wholly to the good. But like all emotions it cannot be produced merely by realizing that it is desirable. It can, I think, be promoted by a manner of life, and by wisdom in education. But that is a matter which I will go into in another chapter. What I am concerned with in this chapter is the element of fear in what is sometimes mistakenly called love. It consists essentially of counsels of prudence, designed to diminish risks from possible retaliation.

I come now to fear as an ingredient in sexual morality. Morality has been concerned always with sex, almost more than with any other topic. There are those, like the Manicheans, who consider sex wicked under all circumstances. But most moral codes have admitted that the human race should be perpetuated, and have therefore been compelled to allow that some forms of sex may be innocent. I think that sexual morality owes its origin to the fear of jealousy. Probably the oldest part of sexual morality is the incest tabu, which is obviously necessary if family life is not to be disrupted by jealousy. In the pre-Christian world, the only other really effective part of sexual morality was the prohibition of adultery with another man's wife. A man was not felt to deserve condemnation for intercourse with unmarried women, unless their fathers were powerful. But intercourse with married women provoked violence on the part of their husbands. The impulse to it was therefore to be feared, and like other impulses causing men to run into danger, it was regarded as a cause of sin. It was prohibited, that is to say, not only because of the violence that it might provoke, but also because the act of adultery was regarded as inherently bad, quite independently of its consequences. This seems to bear out the general view that the impulses which can be labeled as "sinful" are those which cause a man to run into danger, and which therefore he has reason to fear. The whole conception of sin is thus derived from fear of a part of oneself, and represents the conflict between desire and prudence.

We may sum up this discussion by saying that since murder and adultery are alike dangers, the moral law enjoins that you must love your neighbor, but not your neighbor's wife.

Morality, which had its root in rational fears, has always been reinforced by fears which were irrational. There were ghosts; there were demons; there were angry gods. If you had wronged a man who was dead, you might think yourself safe; but no, his ghost would appear at the dead of night and exact retribution. If you had killed a man, you were impure from blood guiltiness, and if your community treated you as if you were guiltless, the gods would be angry with your community. It therefore became to the interest of your community to punish you. But if the person you had killed was someone in whom your community, and therefore its gods, took no particular interest, you were allowed to escape with a comparatively harmless ceremony of purification. Sometimes, however, as in the case of Orestes, when earthly powers were puzzled, supernatural powers took a hand.

Christianity erected this into a dogma. If you committed certain sins and were not purified by repentance and absolution, you suffered eternal torment after death. As we have seen, this might be the penalty for calling your brother a fool. One might have supposed that people who believed this would take care to speak respectfully to their brothers, but experience shows that the belief had no such effect. This is an example of people's inability to act in the manner which they believe the best calculated to promote their own happiness. But the doctrine did have a considerable effect in diminishing the frequency of the more deliberate mortal sins, such as marrying your deceased wife's sister. It must be said, however, that conventional moralists did not rely wholly upon fear of hell. They also invented such maxims as "Honesty is the best policy," which supplied more immediate sanctions for the moral law. But this doctrine, like that of hell fire, is essentially an appeal to fear, and supplies no mechanism except self-control for the production of desirable behavior.

Self-control, though I will not for a moment deny its necessity on occasion, is not the best way of getting people to behave well. It has the drawback of diminishing energy and creativeness. It is like wearing heavy armor, which while it may prevent your arm from striking others, makes it also too heavy to be capable of useful movement. Those who rely wholly upon self-control become stiff and timorous through fear of themselves. But the impulses to which they allow no outlet continue to exist and, like rivers that are dammed, they must overflow sooner or later. Energies which we do not allow their natural outlet in furthering our own life either become atrophied or find an outlet in thwarting the lives of others. They will seek some outlet of this kind which is not dangerous to ourselves, for example, parental tyranny. And when this is not a sufficient outlet, there are other things that can be done. Certain people are condemned as outcasts, whose torture is tolerated by society, and therefore involves no risk. Sometimes these outcasts are criminals, sometimes they are slaves. The criminal law has, from the point of view of thwarted virtue, the merit of allowing an outlet for those impulses of aggression which cowardice, disguised as morality, restrains in their more spontaneous forms. War has the same merit. You must not kill your neighbor, whom perhaps you genuinely hate, but by a little propaganda this hate can be transferred to some foreign nation, against whom all your murderous impulses become patriotic heroism. But there is no deep satisfaction either in torturing criminals or in killing foreigners. For the fundamental impulse is one of hatred of a part of yourself, and the fear which you feel because this part exists.

You will not recover inward harmony by any merely outward acts. Inward harmony is only for those whose impulses are such that they can find constructive, rather than destructive, outlets. The man whose disharmony leads him to devious aggressions against those whom society allows him to think wicked, remains to himself, in the watches of the night, or whenever self-knowledge thrusts itself upon him, a quite different sort of being from the splendid, blustering, swashbuckling hero whom he presents for the public gaze. In the center of his being he feels himself a little frightened man, probably still a child, exposed to reproaches from his father or schoolmaster, or to cold looks from his mother. The more he fears his own dangerous impulses, the more uncomfortable he becomes, and the more he seeks to escape the discomfort by projecting the guilt upon others. His farthest advance in self-knowledge is to say "There, but for the grace of God, go I." But he does not allow himself to doubt the grace of God, for it is the grace of God that allows the little frightened man to feel safe. And when his fright turns to aggression, as fright will, he thinks that the aggression will prosper through God's help.

One of the merits of the moral law is that it gives a set of rules by which it is possible at one and the same time to avoid the hostility of the powerful, and to make hostility against outcasts sufficiently safe even for the most timorous.

The only way to make a fundamental improvement in this psychology of fear, guilt, punishment and retribution, is to create in men, while they are still young, impulses and aptitudes which lead them to a life that does not involve any violent clash with others, because the things that are desired are things in a man's own growth and his own constructive activities, not things which essentially depend upon the thwarting of others.

I think that this principle can be applied also to sexual morality, though there I will admit there are obstacles due partly to nature, and partly to long ages of tradition. Conventional morality approves of jealousy (within limits) since it is a force increasing the danger of the sort of conduct that is reprehended, and therefore serves more immediately and more tangibly the same purposes as are served by hell fire. But jealousy is bound up with possessiveness, and is caused partly by the fear of losing love, partly by the feeling that so long as possession is secure, the presence or absence of love is a matter of indifference. I do not suppose that Solomon expected all his six hundred wives to love him, but he did expect them to be kept safely within the harem as his private possessions. In this extreme form, modern customs no longer sanction jealousy. But the psychological mechanism is still the same. If you are loved you may be thankful, as you would be on a sunny day; if you are not loved, you may well be sad. But you will not secure love by insistence. It may be, if you are unfortunate, that the particular love you have lost may not be recovered, but the world is not lost through one misfortune, and if you realize what it was that caused you to lose love in this case, you may avoid a similar misfortune in a future case. And it may even be that the misfortune will have an effect in opening your heart and mind to new possibilities, and thereby secure for you in the end a freer and happier life than you had supposed possible. To keep a person who does not love you in a prison, whether it be that of a harem or that of social respectability, is not a way to secure anything that a decent person could value. Love is good and cannot be kept alive by being bound in fetters. Jealousy is due to the fear of being unable to retain love, and the cure for this is not to punish those who do not love us, but rather to be lovable. It is open to each one of us to be lovable, and when we fail, it is largely because we have allowed fear to have too great a dominion over us. Consider what makes some children lovable. We love them for their spontaneity, their expansiveness, their joy in living. These things life is only too apt to destroy, and it destroys them most surely when it forbids love. Nevertheless, the Gospels bid us to become as little children, and in the respects that we are thinking of this is a wise precept. Those of us who are no longer young are apt to allow ourselves to become rigid and censorious and morose, and unnecessarily limited in our interests. And if we allow ourselves to be like this, we may find that we are thought unlovable, and if we do not understand rightly what is the matter, this may drive us farther in the very directions which are causing our unhappiness. We can instead seek the outlets that give profound satisfaction, and acquire once more the happy spontaneity of children. We shall then find ourselves less prone to jealousy. We shall realize that it is not by keeping others in prison walls that we shall lead them to love us, but that nevertheless it is within our power to secure love. Love, if it is to be satisfactory, must not be obsessed by the fear of loss. It should rejoice in what the gods give, not destroy the gift by the corroding fear of jealousy.

XVIII

Fortitude

FEAR, which we considered in the last chapter, is the thing which in a wise society would exist rarely because there would be few occasions for feeling it. But in the world in which we are compelled to live at the present time, there are vast occasions for fears which it requires much fortitude to endure. I want in this chapter to consider not how to remove the external occasions for fear, but how to inform and discipline our own minds so that, even when the occasions for fear are present, we may be able to rise above them, and preserve at once equanimity in regard to our own fate and hope in regard to the destiny of mankind.

There is only too much reason to fear that Western civilization, if not the whole world, is likely in the near future to go through a period of immense sorrow and suffering and pain—a period during which, if we are not careful to remember them, the things that we are attempting to preserve may be forgotten in bitterness and poverty and disorder. Courage, hope and unshakable conviction will be necessary if we are to emerge from the dark time spiritually undamaged. It is worth while, before the actual danger is upon us, to collect our thoughts, to marshal our hopes and to plant in our hearts a firm belief in our ideals.

It is not the first time that such disasters have threatened the Western world. The fall of Rome was another such time, and in that time, as now, varying moods of despair, escape and robust faith were exemplified in the writings of leading men. What emerged and became the kernel of the new civilization was the Christian Church. Many pagans were noble in their thoughts and admirable in their aspirations, but they lacked dynamic force.

Plotinus, the founder of Neoplatonism, was the most remarkable of the pagans of that time. In his youth he hoped to play some part in world affairs and accompanied the Emperor in a campaign against Persia, but the Roman soldiers murdered the Emperor and decided to go home. Plotinus found his way home as best he could, and decided to have done with practical affairs.

He then retired into meditation and wrote books full of beauty, extolling the eternal world and the inactive contemplation of it. Such philosophy, however admirable in itself, offered no cure for the ills from which the empire was suffering.

I think Plotinus was right in urging contemplation of eternal things, but he was wrong in thinking of this as enough to constitute a good life. Contemplation, if it is to be wholesome and valuable, must be married to practice: it must inspire action and ennoble the aims of practical statesmanship. While it remains secluded in the cloister it is only a means of escape.

Boethius, who represents the very last blossoming of Roman civilization, was a figure of more use to our age. After a lifetime spent in public administration and in trying to civilize a Gothic king, he fell into disfavor and was condemned to death. In prison he composed his great book, *The Consolations of Philosophy*, in which, with a combination of majestic calm and sweet reasonableness, he sets forth, as imperturbably as though he were still a powerful minister, the joys of contem-

plation, the delight in the beauty of the world and the hopes
for mankind, which, even in that situation, did not desert him.
Throughout the Dark Ages his book was studied and it transmitted to happier times the last purified legacy of the ancient
world.

The sages of our time have a similar duty to perform. It is
their duty to posterity to crystallize the achievements, the
hopes and the ideals which have made our time great—to study
them with monumental simplicity, so that they may shine like
a beacon-light through the coming darkness.

Two very different conceptions of human life are struggling
for mastery of the world. In the West we see man's greatness
in the individual life. A great society for us is one which is
composed of individuals who, as far as is humanly possible,
are happy, free and creative. We do not think that individuals
should be alike. We conceive society as like an orchestra, in
which the different performers have different parts to play
and different instruments upon which to perform, and in
which co-operation results from a conscious common purpose. We believe that each individual should have his proper
pride. He should have his personal conscience and his personal aims, which he should be free to develop except where
they can be shown to cause injury to others. We attach importance to the diminution of suffering and poverty, to the
increase of knowledge and the production of beauty and art.
The State for us is a convenience, not an object of worship.

The Russian Government has a different conception of the
ends of life. The individual is thought to be of no importance;
he is expendable. What is important is the State, which is regarded as something almost divine and having a welfare of its
own not consisting in the welfare of citizens. This view, which
Marx took over from Hegel, is fundamentally opposed to the
Christian ethic, which in the West is accepted by free-thinkers
as much as by Christians. In the Soviet world human dignity

counts for nothing. It is thought right and proper that men should be groveling slaves, bowing down before the semi-divine beings who embody the greatness of the State. When a man betrays his dearest friend and causes him, as a penalty for a moment's indiscretion, to vanish into the mysterious horror of a Siberian labor camp; when a schoolchild, as the result of indoctrination by his teacher, causes his parents to be condemned to death; when a man of exceptional courage, after struggling against evils, is tried, convicted, and abjectly confesses that he has sinned in opposing the Moloch power of the authorities, neither the betrayal nor the confession brings any sense of shame to the perpetrator, for has he not been engaged in the service of his divinity?

It is this conception that we have to fight, a conception which, to my mind and to that of most men who appreciate what the Western world stands for, would, if it prevailed, take everything out of life that gives it value, leaving nothing but a regimented collection of groveling animals. I cannot imagine a greater or more profound cause for which to fight. But if we are to win a victory—not only on the battlefield but in the hearts of men and in the institutions that they support —we must be clear in our own minds as to what it is that we value, and we must, like Boethius, fortify our courage against the threat of adversity.

While Russia underestimates the individual, there are those in the West who unduly magnify the separateness of separate persons. No man's ego should be enclosed in granite walls: its boundaries should be translucent. The first step in wisdom, as well as in morality, is to open the windows of the ego as wide as possible. Most people find little difficulty in including their children within the compass of their desires. In slightly lesser degree they include their friends, and, in time of danger, their country. Very many men feel that what hurts their country hurts them. In 1940 I knew Frenchmen living prosperously in

America who suffered from the fall of France almost as they would have suffered from the loss of a leg. But it is not enough to enlarge our sympathies to embrace our own country. If the world is ever to have peace it will be necessary to learn to embrace the whole human race in the same kind of sympathy which we now feel toward our compatriots. And if we are to retain calm and sanity in difficult times, it is a great help if the furniture of our minds contains past and future ages.

Few things are more purifying to our conception of values than to contemplate the gradual rise of man from his obscure and difficult beginnings to his present eminence. Man, as was said in an earlier chapter, when he first emerged, was a rare and hunted species, not so fleet as the deer, not so nimble as the monkey, unable to defend himself against wild beasts, without the protection of warm fur against rain and cold, living precariously upon the food that he could gather, without weapons, without domestic animals, without agriculture.

The one advantage that he possessed—intelligence—in the end gave him security. He learned the use of fire, of bows and arrows, of language, of domestic animals and, at last, of agriculture. He learned to co-operate in communities, to build great palaces and pyramids, to explore the world in all directions, and, at last, to cope with disease and poverty. He studied the stars, he invented geometry, and he learned to substitute machines for muscles in necessary labor. Some of the most important of these advances are very recent and are as yet confined to Western nations.

We of the Western world, faced with Communism's hostile criticism, have been too modest and too defensive in our attitude. Throughout the long ages since life began, to repeat what was said earlier, the mechanism of evolution has involved cruel suffering, endless struggle for bare subsistence, and in the end, in most cases, death by starvation. This is the law in the animal kingdom, and it remained until the present century the law among human beings also. Now, at last, certain nations have discovered how to prevent abject poverty, how to prevent the pain and sorrow and waste of useless births condemned to premature death, and how to substitute intelligence and care for the blind ruthlessness of nature.

The nations that have made this discovery are trustees for the future of mankind. They must have the courage of their new way of life and not allow themselves to be bemused or bewildered by the slogans of the semi-civilized. We have a right to hopes that are rational, that can be itemized and set forth in statistics. If we allow ourselves to be robbed of these hopes for the sake of irrational dreams, we shall be traitors to the human race.

If bad times lie ahead of us we should remember while they last the slow march of man, checkered in the past by devastations and retrogressions, but always resuming the movement toward progress. Spinoza, who was one of the wisest of men and who lived consistently in accordance with his own wisdom, advised men to view passing events "under the aspect of eternity." Those who can learn to do this will find a painful present much more bearable than it would otherwise be. They can see it as a passing moment—a discord to be resolved, a tunnel to be traversed. The small child who has hurt himself weeps as if the world contained nothing but sorrow, because his mind is confined to the present. A man who has learned wisdom from Spinoza can see even a lifetime of suffering as a passing moment in the life of humanity. And the human race itself, from its obscure beginning to its unknown end, is only a minute episode in the life of the universe.

What may be happening elsewhere we do not know, but it is improbable that the universe contains nothing better than ourselves. With increase of wisdom our thoughts acquire a wider scope both in space and in time. The child lives in the minute, the boy in the day, the instinctive man in the year.

The man imbued with history lives in the epoch. Spinoza would have us live not in the minute, the day, the year or the epoch, but in eternity. Those who learn to do this will find that it takes away the frantic quality of misfortune and prevents the trend towards madness that comes with overwhelming disaster. Spinoza spent the last day of his life telling cheerful anecdotes to his host. He had written: "A free man thinks of death least of all things, and his wisdom is a meditation not of death but of life." And he carried out this precept when it came to his own death.

I do not mean that the man who is freed from the tyranny of unwisdom will be destitute of emotion—on the contrary, he will feel friendship, benevolence and compassion in a higher degree than the man who has not emancipated himself from personal anxieties. His ego will not be a wall between him and the rest of mankind. He will feel, like Buddha, that he cannot be completely happy while anybody is miserable. He will feel pain—a wider and more diffused pain than that of the egoist—but he will not find the pain unendurable. He will not be driven by it to invent comfortable fairy tales which assure him that the sufferings of others are illusory. He will not lose poise and self-control. Like Milton's Satan he will say:

> The mind is its own place, and in itself
> Can make a Heav'n of Hell, a Hell of Heav'n.

Above all, he will remember that each generation is trustee to future generations of the mental and moral treasure that man has accumulated through the ages. It is easy to forget the glory of man. When King Lear is going mad he meets Edgar, who pretends to be mad and wears only a blanket. King Lear moralizes: "Unaccommodated, man is no more but such a poor, bare, forked animal as thou art."

This is half of the truth. The other half is uttered by Hamlet:

What a piece of work is man! how noble in reason! how infinite in faculty! In form and moving how express and admirable! in action how like an angel! in apprehension how like a god!

Soviet man, crawling on his knees to betray his friends and family to slow butchery, is hardly worthy of Hamlet's words, but it is possible to be worthy of them. It is possible for every one of us. Every one of us can enlarge his mind, release his imagination and spread wide his affection and benevolence. And it is those who do this whom ultimately mankind reveres. The East reveres Buddha, the West reveres Christ. Both taught love as the secret of wisdom. The earthly life of Christ was contemporary with that of the Emperor Tiberius, who spent his life in cruelty and disgusting debauchery. Tiberius had pomp and power: in his day millions trembled at his nod. But he is forgotten except by historians.

Those who live nobly, even if in their day they live obscurely, need not fear that they will have lived in vain. Something radiates from their lives, some light that shows the way to their friends, their neighbors, perhaps to long future ages. I find many men nowadays oppressed with a sense of impotence, with the feeling that in the vastness of modern societies there is nothing of importance that the individual can do. This is a mistake. The individual, if he is filled with love of mankind, with breadth of vision, with courage and with endurance, can do a great deal.

As geological time goes, it is but a moment since the human race began, and only the twinkling of an eye since the arts of civilization were first invented. In spite of some alarmists, it is hardly likely that our species will completely exterminate itself. And so long as man continues to exist, we may be pretty sure that, whatever he may suffer for a time, and whatever brightness may be eclipsed, he will emerge sooner or later, perhaps strengthened and reinvigorated by a period of mental sleep. The universe is vast and men are but tiny specks on an insignificant planet. But the more we realize our minuteness and our impotence in the face of cosmic forces, the more astonishing becomes what human beings have achieved.

It is to the possible achievements of man that our ultimate loyalty is due, and in that thought the brief troubles of our unquiet epoch become endurable. Much wisdom remains to be learned, and if it is only to be learned through adversity, we must endeavor to endure adversity with what fortitude we can command. But if we can acquire wisdom soon enough, adversity may not be necessary and the future of man may be happier than any part of his past.

XIX

Life Without Fear

THE thing that above all others I have been concerned to say in this book is that because of fears that once had a rational basis mankind has failed to profit by the new techniques that, if wisely used, could make him happy. Fear makes man unwise in the three great departments of human conduct: his dealings with nature, his dealings with other men, and his dealings with himself. I wish in this chapter to consider the ways in which the world would be better if we were exempt from the tyranny of ancient fears.

It is necessary first of all to distinguish between fear as an emotion and rational apprehension of danger as a piece of knowledge. It would be foolish to be unaware of dangers when they exist, but it is very seldom that a danger can be dealt with as adequately by fear as by rational apprehension. Fear is a reaction which we share with the animals. It is crude and slapdash. Sometimes it serves the purposes of self-preservation, but sometimes it does quite the opposite. The man who is not mastered by fear is much better able to think out what kind of action will minimize the danger. Fear frequently prevents people from admitting the danger which in fact they are fearing, and therefore causes them not to take precautions that wisdom would advise. Sometimes this takes very absurd forms, as, for example, when fear of death prevents a man from making a will. It is important to make this point clear, since otherwise it might be thought that in speaking against fear one is speaking against a clear view of real perils.

Different kinds of dangers need different kinds of treatment. There are limitations to which human beings are subject owing to the physical facts of nature. These limitations are to a certain degree unavoidable, and to that degree must be accepted. On the other hand, the obstacles to well-being which arise from our relations to other people or to ourselves are to a very great extent unnecessary. There is nothing unavoidable about the misery that people cause each other through hatred or ill-will, nor about the misery that they cause themselves from a sense of guilt. Methods of dealing with the different kinds of evils are for this reason very different.

The limitations imposed by nature have to do with food and raw materials and with the physiological fact of death. These are not absolute; by more labor it is possible to produce more food, and by better technique it is possible to economize raw materials or make use of new substances that were previously thought worthless. Death can be postponed by medicine and wise living. But in all these three respects, although we cannot place an exact limit at one precise point, limits do exist. No amount of medicine will make a man immortal, and no amount of science could provide food if there were only standing room for the population. These limitations that are imposed by nature must be considered scientifically, in order that they may be met in the manner that will involve the smallest amount of suffering. In regard to food, as I have pointed out in previous chapters, the solution lies in birth-control; as regards raw materials, the solution will lie partly in a more scientific technique and partly in international control to prevent waste and secure just distribution; the postponement of death is a medical matter, but willing submission to it is a matter of psychology to which I shall return later.

In the past, the limitations imposed by nature have been dealt with superstitiously. There were gods or demons, or witches capable of invoking evil spirits, and if they were not placated, they caused bad weather. To this day, archbishops think that drought or excessive rain should be dealt with by prayer. Very often the methods demanded by superstition aggravate the evil. In the Middle Ages when there was a plague the population were encouraged to assemble in churches to pray; this, of course, provided an ideal method of spreading infection. Such evils, so far as they can be eradicated, can be eradicated only by science. The scientific attitude has the twofold merit of causing willingness to admit the evil and intelligence in the search for means of mitigating it. There are still many evils in the world, of which overpopulation is perhaps the most menacing, in regard to which a large proportion of even the most civilized nations are wholly unscientific.

Fear of other human beings in the world as we have known it is often well-founded, in the sense that there are those who will injure us if they can. But even when this is the case, it is not by fear, as a rule, that those who wish us ill can be best prevented from injuring us. If you have ever owned a dog that had a propensity to pursue sheep, you will have noticed that although he may remain well behaved so long as the sheep are stationary, he cannot resist temptation if they begin to run away. In this respect many of us are like the dog and many of us like the sheep. I once observed a purely psychological encounter between a Great Dane and a kitten three weeks old. The kitten stayed its ground, and spat and bristled and hissed. What went on in the mind of the Great Dane I do not know, but he behaved as if he thought the kitten had supernatural protection. After staring for a while, he put his tail between his legs and slunk away. If you have as much courage as this kitten, you will find it capable of protecting you against a great deal of aggression from which you might otherwise suffer. But this sort of behavior is all within the capacity of animals, and I am more concerned with the sort of behavior of which only human beings are capable. A great deal of the aggressiveness in the world is inspired by fear. We bark at our neighbor for fear that he will attack us, and he barks at us for the same reason. It happens not infrequently that you can cure aggressiveness by a display of friendliness. This is the element of truth in the doctrine of non-resistance, a doctrine which in its theoretical and absolute form I cannot accept, but which certainly contains a larger proportion of practical wisdom than most people would suppose. I think that every individual who does not display aggressive impulses does something to diminish some of such impulses in others. Even a mere external code of manners has its good effect in this respect, but when the non-aggressiveness is deeply rooted in character its effect is very much greater than it can ever be when it springs from a mere conventional rule.

Whenever a fear is well-grounded in the sense that the danger apprehended is real, there are two different things that need to be done: one is to create in the individual that kind of fortitude that makes him able to face possible misfortunes calmly, and the other is to ameliorate the social system in such a way as to cause the danger to disappear. This applies, for example, to the fear of destitution, which is very widespread and very deep-seated in all competitive countries. A very great many people who seem otherwise sane are quite irrational about money. There are men who, though they are willing to write large checks, cannot bear to part with loose cash, and rather than do so will face black looks from untipped waiters. Arnold Bennett's Clayhanger, throughout a completely successful business career, continues to be haunted by fear of the workhouse. To prevent such fears there are three different sorts of things to be done. There is first the purely Stoic method of persuading a man that he should face misfortune calmly, and not let himself mind too much even when misfortunes occur. The supreme example of this is Milton's Satan. Then there is the method of persuading him that he is not very likely to become destitute; in mild cases this may be done by economic arguments, but in extreme cases it is a matter for the psychiatrist. Lastly there is the political method of coping with the whole problem of destitution, and making it no longer one of the things that befall the unfortunate. All these methods should be pursued in all such cases. The Stoic method is admirable when nothing better is possible, but although a man may face misfortune bravely, it would still be better if he did not have to face it. And it is clear that fear, when it exists to a morbid degree, is a product of a society in which real misfortunes are not unusual. Methods which deal only with the individual, therefore, useful as they may be, can never be substitutes for methods that remove the evil wholly by political means. It is important to realize this, for there are those who have so passionate an admiration for courage that they rejoice in opportunities for its exercise. This is absurd. You may admire a man who endures a long and painful illness without repining, but clearly it would be better if he enjoyed good health. You may admire a soldier who dies nobly in battle, but it would be much better if he did not die. In this respect the Stoics were to blame, since they praised endurance so much as to make cruelty seem almost a good thing, for cruelty was a necessary means to what they considered the highest good. It used to be a custom to praise the patient endurance of the poor, but that was before they had the vote.

Social dealings in private life are filled with fear, especially in Britain. People take pains not to wear their heart on their sleeves for daws to peck at. As far as they can, they keep their emotions to themselves. They will behave in exactly the same way to you whether they like you or dislike you, provided they have no motive of self-interest for making up to you. They are stiff and shy and unspontaneous. They wear an armor designed to conceal the frightened child within. The result is that social intercourse becomes boring, that friendships have little life in them, and that love is only a pale shadow of what it might be. People quote with approval Browning's remark:

> God be thanked, the meanest of his creatures
> Boasts two soul-sides, one to face the world with,
> One to show a woman when he loves her.

I am not a psychoanalyst, but I think that if I were I could find something to say about Browning's thankfulness on this point. The side that he faces the world with is the one that he feels he can exploit without the fear of being hurt, the one that gives no handle for ridicule and no knowledge that may be used to inflict pain; the other "soul-side," the one that he shows a woman when he loves her, contains all the vanity and conceit and bombast that he dare not show to the men at his club. It is almost as much a product of fear as the other, because the other prevents him from letting fresh air into the inner chambers of his ego, and no one can be admitted to these inner chambers except in a relation of mutual adulation. The outer world is bleak, the inner world is stuffy. This is not how human relations should be. They should be free and spontaneous. Vanity should be less touchy and envy less widespread. The habit of reserve not only makes it easy for self-deception to flourish secretly, but also, owing to the energy spent in the purely negative occupation of preventing self-expression, greatly diminishes the fruitful outflow of energy in useful ways. It has the further defect that men are particularly anxious to conceal friendly impulses, since these especially, if known, make them feel that they are vulnerable. Hours of tedium and years of ossification result from this reign of social terror.

I do not imagine a world without fear as an anarchic world. There will be freedom in certain directions in which now freedom is much restricted, but in other directions where now there is freedom there will instead be law. There will be laws regulating the food supply and the distribution of raw materials. Above all, there will have to be laws for the prevention of war. I think, also, that it is impossible to have a world in which there is much freedom without excessive anarchy unless certain things are taught in the process of education. Where man's relation to physical nature is concerned, there is to be scientific discipline, that is to say, a habit of trying to ascertain the facts and admitting them when they have been ascertained. The world at present is full of sentimentalists who, when they find a fact unpleasant, merely refuse to admit that it is a fact. This habit of mind is capable of doing untold harm, because the unpleasant facts will have their unpleasant effects all the more fully for having been not recognized. Intellectual discipline, in the sense of willingness to admit facts, should result from education. It is merely stupid not to acknowledge the power of nature in so far as this power exists. Any attempt at self-assertion in this sphere is a failure of sanity.

Owing to the power of physical nature, certain habits, which only education is likely to create, are very useful for survival. I do not believe that any child brought up without discipline will brush its teeth. Indeed it is unlikely that the child will be sufficiently cleanly in its habits to be free from vermin. The preservation of health demands physical discipline which it is is not likely that children will acquire through mere exhortations addressed to self-interest in later years. I think a certain amount of discipline in education is necessary, not only for reasons of health, but also to produce those habits of social behavior which make perpetual quarreling unnecessary. We do not at mealtimes snatch the food from our neighbor, but the reason that we do not is that we were taught not to at a very early age. Long before we are grown up, the habit has become so engrained that we have ceased to be conscious of it. Punctuality at meals, though it is a tedious virtue, is important, since it minimizes the amount of service required. For such reasons, I think that habit-formation must be an important part of early education. Some modern educators have perhaps carried freedom in education somewhat too far in this respect. There is, however, a kind of freedom which education should preserve, though it seldom does so. I am thinking of emotional freedom. The reasons in favor of emotional freedom are various: on the one hand, too much control over the emotions is deadening, and causes loss of vitality; on the other hand, emotions which are not allowed an outlet turn bad, and find other outlets much more harmful than those that have been forbidden. There is also a third reason, which is that wherever a society is much bound by conventional rules, many emotions will be considered undesirable which in fact are harmless. I think, therefore, that while discipline is necessary in regard to scientific fact and in regard to certain habits without which social life becomes difficult, there should in education be as little as possible of discipline over the emotions. Above all, there must never be any attempt to cause the expression of emotions which are likely to be insincere.

Educators in the past tended too much to believe in original sin, and to think that the child ought to be made into something quite different from what nature would make it. The extreme example of this occurs in St. Augustine's account of his learning Latin and Greek. Latin, he says, he learned without difficulty at his mother's knee, and, of course, in the end he knew it well; Greek he learned from a cruel schoolmaster with many beatings and much harshness, and with the result, so he tells us, that he never knew it well. Nevertheless, he thinks better of the method by which he was taught Greek, for this, he says, cured him of "pernicious blithesomeness." This is the exact antithesis of what an educator ought to feel. An educator should think of a child as a gardener thinks of a plant, as something to be made to grow by having the right soil and the right amount of water. If your roses fail to bloom, it does not occur to you to whip them, but you try to find out what has been amiss in your treatment of them. If your children fail to bloom, you should treat them as you would the roses. With few exceptions, what is wanted is positive, not negative. The important thing is what the children do, not what they do not do. And what they do, if it is to have value, must be a spontaneous expression of their own vital energy. You can, if you think fit, prepare children for a military life by teaching them all to do the same thing at the same moment when they hear the word of command. If you do, they will grow up thwarted and stunted and full of a deep-seated anger against the world—no doubt useful emotions if they are to be soldiers employed in killing, but not if they are to be happy citizens of a world at peace.

The Happy Man

I WANT to describe in this chapter the way that I imagine the life and temperament of ordinary men in the society that we could create if we chose. In the world as it is at present only those who are exceptionally fortunate can live in the way that I shall describe, and practically nobody can live in this way in time of war. But in what I shall say I shall assume nothing that need in future be exceptional.

The happy man will have in childhood parents who are fond of him. He will be more likely to get affection from his parents than he is at present, because their affections will be freer and their anxieties will be less, and because they will regard parenthood as a partnership in the bringing up of children, not as a sexual prison. In childhood, his environment will be such that it is much less often necessary to say "don't" than it is at present. He should spend most of the daytime hours in large playrooms with other children, or out of doors if the weather is suitable. During these hours he should not be surrounded by valuable but fragile objects which he must not touch. The walls should not be so exquisitely colored that on no account must dirty fingermarks appear upon them. The playroom should be sufficiently remote from other people for it to be unnecessary to tell children not to make a noise.

Everything must be on one level so that there are no steps upon which they can hurt themselves. There must, of course, be no knives or other sharp instruments within their reach. In such an environment a great many "don'ts" which are unavoidable in a small home will become unnecessary. I do not pretend that there will be no prohibitions. Children will have to be prevented from ill-treating each other, but, as far as possible, this should be done by keeping them interested in some activity which they enjoy, rather than by restraining bullying impulses by direct authority.

The framework of life in childhood should have a routine which is only varied on great occasions, such as holidays or expeditions. The child needs two things above all else: one is freedom to grow, and the other is security. Security comes to children from affection and routine. They do not feel secure unless they know more or less what to expect. Although children should not be surrounded by tabus, they should not be left entirely to their own devices. Intelligent adults should suggest occupations that children will like, and should have the art of suggesting them in a tone of voice that inclines children to say "yes" rather than "no." I think by this means a child can reach school age without being filled with complexes, fears, and furies.

Scholastic education is a tiresome necessity. I can remember a feeling of profound regret when my children, after playing on the beach all day long, reached the age at which they had to be taught to read and write. I should have liked to leave them to grow freely in the enjoyment of sea and sun, but civilization depends upon difficult and complex habits which are not to be acquired without a certain amount of sitting still. But although I do not think that scholastic education can be entirely free from irksome slavery, it can be much more nearly free than it is where conventional methods are employed. Intelligent children, if they are not prematurely forced, can learn to read and write because they want to. For children whose natural bent is manual rather than verbal, conventional education is much too passive.

In classical Greece, "gentlemen" did nothing with their hands because they had slaves. On the other hand, they spent a very great deal of time talking. Their houses were not full of gadgets, as our houses are, and there was hardly anything in their civilization that was not a suitable subject for conversation at a dinner-table. Snobbery ever since has made them the pattern that educators imitate. When you have taken a First in Greats at Oxford, you can talk and write about anything that would have interested Sophocles or Plato, but you do not know how the telephone or the electric light works. You are unaware of the mechanism of combustion, and practically the whole material apparatus of the civilization that you enjoy is unintelligible to you, because it did not exist in the time of Pericles. And owing to the nature of scholastic education, the young people who win distinction are those whose tastes are verbal. The boy whose tastes are manual, although when he grows up he is likely to be able to do something more useful than writing a leading article, wins less respect than his more literary contemporary. This, at least, is the case in Europe; in America things are rather different. Boys whose tastes are manual rather than verbal are the great majority, and their education ought to be more in workshops than at desks. It would not be difficult to make them aware of the necessity of some scholastic education as a necessary tool in the perfection of manual accomplishment. All education can be pleasant if the child feels that it is important. It only becomes drudgery when it appears pointless to the child, and very often when this is the case, the child is right and the teacher wrong. I think, therefore, that although some drudgery is unavoidable in the production of an educated adult, there need be very much less than is usually thought, especially if people have a more modern conception of what it is to be educated.

I do not suggest that the cultural side of education should be ignored. I think, on the contrary, that it is essential to the production of the sort of adult who best fits the modern world. But I think that what is important in cultural education should be conveyed, at any rate in the early stages, by methods far more attractive than those now usual. History and geography should be taught at first by means of the cinema. When taught in this way, they will give pleasure, attention will be spontaneous and therefore the impression will be less temporary. In spite of reforming movements, there is still among educators too much of St. Augustine's feeling that education should cure "pernicious blithesomeness," and that what is enjoyed without effort cannot have much educational value. I think this is the contrary of the truth. I should have children learn through the cinema the whole epic panorama from Pithecanthropus to the White House. I would have children made aware in the same way of the manners and customs of tribes and nations utterly remote from their own. I would have them, when they happen to meet a Zulu, not feel that he is something strange and remote, but think to themselves "Ah yes, I know how he behaves because I saw a movie about him." Education, conducted on these lines, would do more than many books to cure provincialism in space and time, and to make children realize that actual human beings with actual feelings can be outwardly very different from the people among whom they live, but inwardly composed of the same human material. Those who have a taste for history will proceed afterwards to read books on the subject, but those who have not this scholastic taste will still have benefited by what they have seen on the screen.

Similar principles apply to the artistic side of education. Opportunities for literature, music and painting should be given to those who like them, but nobody should be made to drudge at them. Their purpose is to give pleasure, and it is a shocking sight to see disciplinarians making them into a means of torture. Children are made to learn bits of Shakespeare by heart, with the result that ever after they associate him with pedantic boredom. If they could meet him in the flesh, full of jollity and ale, they would be astonished, and if they had never heard of him before they might be led by his jollity to see what he had written. But if at school they had been inoculated against him, they will never be able to enjoy him. The same sort of thing applies to music lessons. Human beings have certain capacities for spontaneous enjoyment, but moralists and pedants possess themselves of the apparatus of these enjoyments, and having extracted what they consider the poison of pleasure they leave them dreary and dismal and devoid of everything that gives them value. Shakespeare did not write with a view to boring school-children; he wrote with a view to delighting his audiences. If he does not give you delight, you had better ignore him.

In Europe, though not in America, the abler children have their lives ruined by anxiety and fatigue in the competition for scholarships. Many break down at the university, many others as soon as their university career is ended. This system is cruel, and is also a waste of valuable material. It is necessitated in Europe by lack of funds. Some method has to be found of deciding who shall have a university education, but the scholarship method is ideally wrong, since it ensures that a large proportion of those who succeed in examinations are ruined by the severity of the struggle. This is part and parcel of the financial stringency dictated by the supposed necessity of preferring guns to butter, and only secure world peace can afford a fundamental remedy.

The happy man, as I conceive him in the society of the future, will have as much scholastic education as he chooses, without regard to ability in examinations. Most people who have little scholastic ability have also little taste for scholastic pursuits, and few of them would wish to continue such pursuits after the age of 21.

In every society, however Utopian, every healthy adult will be expected to do some kind of useful work. I think there should be opportunities for those who have exceptional tastes to work half-time for half-pay. This is important because the very best work is usually considered worthless by contemporaries, and it must be possible for a man to devote a part of his time to things that others do not think worth doing. Such men, however, will be exceptional; for others it would be possible, given a sensible economic organization, for them to be secure of a livelihood by, say, six hours' work a day. This is, in fact, no hardship, for idleness is not a road to happiness. There should be economic security for all who are not idle, and even for those who are, if they are idle through no fault of their own.

In personal relations, the happy man, having been brought up in youth without the twin obsessions of sin and fear, will be free and generous and expansive, regarding other people, except where there is some definite reason to the contrary, as people with whom he co-operates rather than as competitors.

He will not be constantly inhibiting impulses to friendliness for fear lest others should take advantage of him or should fail to respond. His attitude to others will be far more trustful than is common in the present day, and in nine cases out of ten the fact that this is his attitude will bring about a response that justifies it. Having learned while he was young the economics and politics of co-operation, and the habit of regarding the human family as one, he will not instinctively think of foreign nations as enemies, and he will see war as the folly that it is.

Inventors of Utopias usually make them intolerably dull,

because their main preoccupation is with security. A happy man needs opportunities of adventure almost as much as he needs security. He needs security in the general framework of his life, but he needs adventure to give excitement and to enable him to savor the security when he returns to it. Modern life, owing partly to machine production and partly to economic insecurity, leaves little opportunity for adventure in the lives of the majority of mankind. But this is unnecessary. It should be possible for a man, if he feels so disposed, to save out of his earnings until he is in a position to travel to the Antarctic, or to kill lions in Africa, or to cross the Atlantic in an open boat, or indulge whatever other whim may seize him, provided always that it is not one consisting in injury to others. Even as things are, opportunities for adventure exist for those who feel sufficiently adventurous. This is illustrated by two recent books, *The Kon-Tiki Expedition* and John Caldwell's *Desperate Voyage*. But at present a man requires a rare amount of determination if he is to indulge in such dangerous sports. If the need for adventure were more recognized, opportunities could easily be made more available and more frequent. The same type of man who may now become a gangster or a dictator would probably find his adventurous impulses sufficiently satisfied by conflicts with nature which would do no harm to anyone, and might even happen to be useful, though this should not be regarded as their purpose.

I want to insist once more that the happy man, as I conceive him, is happy, not only owing to the outward circumstances of his adult life, but also owing to a happy temperament which he will owe to the wisdom and kindness of those with whom he spends his first years. Given this kind of temperament, and given an economic system which affords him security, he will be able to enjoy work, to have many friends, to feel affection towards his children, and to pass through the middle years of his life without the sense of frustration and failure that is all too common among middle-aged men in the world as it is. When at last he reaches old age he will look back upon his life without remorse or undue regrets.

The art of growing old is one which the passage of time has forced upon my attention. Psychologically there are two dangers to be guarded against in old age. One of these is undue absorption in the past. It does not do to live in memories, in regrets for the good old days, or in sadness about friends who are dead. One's thoughts must be directed to the future, and to things about which there is something to be done. This is not always easy; one's own past is a gradually increasing weight. It is easy to think to oneself that one's emotions used to be more vivid than they are, and one's mind more keen. If this is true it should be forgotten, and if it is forgotten it will probably not be true.

The other thing to be avoided is clinging to youth in the hope of sucking vigor from its vitality. When your children are grown up they want to live their own lives, and if you continue to be as interested in them as you were when they were young, you are likely to become a burden to them, unless they are unusually callous. I do not mean that one should be without interest in them, but one's interest should be contemplative and, if possible, philanthropic, but not unduly emotional. Animals become indifferent to their young as soon as their young can look after themselves, but human beings, owing to the length of infancy, find this difficult.

I think that a successful old age is easiest for those who have strong impersonal interests involving appropriate activities. It is in this sphere that long experience is really fruitful, and it is in this sphere that the wisdom born of experience can be exercised without being oppressive. It is no use telling grown-up children not to make mistakes, both because they will not believe you, and because mistakes are an essential part of education. But if you are one of those who are incapable of impersonal interests, you may find that your life will be empty unless you concern yourself with your children and grandchildren. In that case you must realize that while you can still render them material services, such as making them an allowance or knitting them jumpers, you must not expect that they will enjoy your company.

Some old people are oppressed by the fear of death. In the young there is a justification for this feeling. Young men who have reason to fear that they will be killed in battle may justifiably feel bitter in the thought that they have been cheated of the best things that life has to offer. But in an old man who has known human joys and sorrows, and has achieved whatever work it was in him to do, the fear of death is somewhat abject and ignoble. The best way to overcome it—so at least it seems to me—is to make your interests gradually wider and more impersonal, until bit by bit the walls of the ego recede, and your life becomes increasingly merged in the universal life. An individual human existence should be like a river—small at first, narrowly contained within its banks, and rushing passionately past boulders and over waterfalls. Gradually the river grows wider, the banks recede, the waters flow more quietly, and in the end, without any visible break, they become merged in the sea, and painlessly lose their individual being. The man who, in old age, can see his life in this way, will not suffer from the fear of death, since the things he cares for will continue. And if, with the decay of vitality, weariness increases, the thought of rest will be not unwelcome. The wise man should wish to die while still at work, knowing that others will carry on what he can no longer do, and content in the thought that what was possible has been done.

The Happy World

I HAVE been concerned in this book to set forth certain facts, and certain hopes which these facts render rational. The facts concern the unification of mankind through modern technique, and the liberation of mankind from bondage to excessive toil which the inadequate techniques of the past rendered unavoidable. The hopes that are based upon these facts are hopes as to the general well-being that may be realized if mankind learned to practice the co-operation which modern techniques demand. There are, it is true, correlative fears, for which there is perhaps as good basis in the present state of the world as for the hopes that I have been setting forth. The technical unification of the world not only makes possible much greater general well-being than at any former time, if it is accompanied by economic and political unification; it also makes possible greater disasters than any known to even the worst of former times, if our technical skill continues to be devoted to disunity rather than unity. I have not, however, in this book dwelt much upon the reasons for fear, since I do not think that it is through fear that we shall avoid the dangers that threaten us. Our world has too much of fear, and emphasis upon dangers is apt to lead to apathetic despair. What our world needs is the opposite; it needs rational creative hope; it needs something positive to live for. It needs "yes" feelings rather than "no" feelings. If the "yes" feelings are as strong as a purely rational consideration allows them to be, the "no" feelings will melt away and become unnecessary. But if we dwell upon "no" feelings too much, we shall never emerge from despair.

I shall assume in what follows that mankind, whether through the lessons of a third world war or through some less painful process, will have come to understand the community of interest which unites the human family. And I shall try to portray the kind of world that will result from this understanding. I shall consider what public institutions can do to bring about a happy issue in the three age-long conflicts of men: with nature, with each other, and with themselves.

Let us begin with the conflict with nature.

There will have to be an international authority controlling the production and distribution of food and raw materials. This authority must have power to prevent such wasteful agricultural methods as have produced the deserts in North Africa and the Dust Bowl in the United States. The present cultivators of the soil must not be allowed to enrich themselves by using up wastefully the natural capital upon which future generations will have to subsist. It must come to be realized that whoever destroys the fertility of the soil in any region is doing an injury to mankind as a whole, and that this is not the sort of injury that private persons, or even whole nations, have a right to inflict. The agricultural authority, in addition to insisting upon soil conservation, will have to give advice on scientific agriculture and to make all knowledge on this subject easily available to every cultivator. But I do not think that cultivators need be *compelled* to adopt the latest scientific methods, except in cases where the old methods are permanently destructive to fertility.

Somewhat similar considerations apply to raw materials.

As I write a dangerous dispute is in progress concerning Iranian oil. The Persians say that it belongs to them, the British and Americans say that it belongs to them, the Russians, in the background, are hoping that it will soon belong to them. But by what right should it belong to any of these contending parties? It was not they who put it there, and it is not they alone who will use it. It should be viewed as the common property of all nations. Socialists have become aware of the evils of private property in land, when the private landowner is a citizen whose interests may be opposed to those of other citizens of his State, but they have not yet become aware of the evils of national private property—I mean property vested in one nation to the exclusion of others. With the unification of world economy, this kind of private property becomes increasingly harmful, and is a constant incentive to war. It is because of this kind of private property that Czechoslovakia has to have a Communist Government, since otherwise Russia would not be able to use its uranium in the manufacture of atom-bombs. For such reasons it is not enough that raw materials should be nationalized; they must be internationalized, and rationed to possible users on some system that has international sanction.

As we have seen, the problem of adequately nourishing the human family cannot be solved while the population continues to increase rapidly. Rapid increase has been checked in the past by famine and pestilence, but these are painful methods. Moreover, their effectiveness is diminishing; medicine is coping with pestilence, and philanthropy is causing famine to be a less localized phenomenon than it used to be. The population problem, therefore, if the world is to flourish in spite of scientific medicine and economic justice, must be dealt with by means of universal birth-control. Whatever this may involve in the way of education, industrialization and increase of prosperity in the poorer regions of the world must be undertaken at no matter what cost, if a scientifically unified world is to be stable, and is not to sink to continually lower levels of subsistence.

I come now to the conflicts of man with man. Here the first thing to be coped with is war. While mankind is subject to the threat of war, especially by the deadly methods which science is perfecting, nothing good can be secure. There is only one way of making the world safe against war, and that is to have only one armed force in the world. There might be local police forces with minor weapons such as could cope with unarmed civilians, but all the really serious weapons of war must be concentrated in the hands of one single authority. When this has been achieved, there will no longer be danger of serious wars, unless they were to take the form of civil wars between different parts of the international force. To prevent this, measures which are not purely military will be required. There will need to be control over education, in the sense that no country must be allowed in its schools to teach a predatory nationalism. The teaching of history everywhere should lay more stress upon the progress of man than upon national victories or defeats in contests with other nations. The books used in the teaching of history should everywhere be such as have been sanctioned by the international authority, and have been certified to be free from nationalistic falsehoods. There should also be a very widely diffused teaching of sound economics—the economics, I mean, which emphasizes the much greater part played by co-operation than by competition in an intelligent modern technique. There should be a gradual approach to universal free trade. There should be complete freedom of travel, as there was in most countries before 1914. There should be interchanges of students, so that many people, while still young enough to be not hardened in habits and prejudices, should become intimate with people of other countries and with their ways of thought and behavior.

The edifice of internationalism in education should have at its apex an international university, open to able students from all countries, containing professors to whom the international ideal appeared important, and affording a refuge to able men who, like Einstein, were found displeasing to their compatriots, for reasons disgraceful to those compatriots. One might hope that in such a university a free community might grow up of men capable, not only of overcoming nationalism in their thoughts by deliberate effort, but of genuinely feeling the unity of man and of the common tasks to which a wise humanity should devote itself.

I come last to the protection of the individual, both against the hostility of the herd and against his own fears. These two are more closely connected than is sometimes thought, for herd hostility is usually the result of fear, and the fear that it expresses, though nominally directed outwards, has, as a rule, its root in a fear which the intolerant individuals feel of a part of themselves. I have spoken in previous chapters of what education in the very early years can do to prevent the growth of underground terrors, such as psychoanalysis lays bare. Affection and security are what is mainly needed in the early years. A population wisely handled in youth will be less liable to herd hostilities than is now common in most parts of the world. Nevertheless, it must be expected that herd hostilities will be sometimes aroused in cases in which to the outsider there seems no just ground for such hostilities. The best way of dealing with such cases would be to provide places of sanctuary, as was done in the Middle Ages; those who had fled to such places should be examined by a neutral authority and should be protected if that authority pronounced them blameless.

Regimentation and uniformity are dangers that an organized industrial world will have to fear, and against which it should take deliberate measures. There should be opportunities for exceptional individuals, such as poets and artists, who would be likely to fail in any attempt to win the approval of elderly bureaucrats. I should have academies for such men, not as a reward for achieved eminence, for then it is too late, but as expressing the favorable opinion of young men engaged in similar pursuits. I would have election to such academies only possible for men under twenty-five, and I would confine the voting for election to members of the Academy concerned who were still under thirty-five. Such regulations might make it possible for the academy not to become an ossified collection of old fogies, as academies too often are.

There would still be some whose work would be too anarchic or too much opposed to the fashion to win the approval even of the young. Blake, for example, would not have secured the suffrages of contemporary poets or painters. Such men would have to make their living by work that left them a certain amount of leisure, and if they were content to live simply this should be possible. There should be for everybody considerably shorter hours of work than are now customary, and much longer holidays than are now enjoyed by anybody except university professors. Some people are afraid that in such a community life would be too tame and unadventurous, but this need not be the case. There are innumerable forms of adventure which could be open to everybody who desired them, if holidays were as long as they easily might be. For those who wish at all times to live strenuously, and to whom a soft life feels disgusting, it should be possible to find a quite sufficient outlet in some really difficult work, whether of artistic creation or of scientific research. Such work stretches men's powers to the very utmost, as much in its way as an attempt to climb Everest; but for those who do not find it adequate, Everest still remains to be conquered.

Unusual individuals whom subsequent ages, but not their contemporaries, have regarded as meritorious, have been possible in the past if they had the good fortune to inherit money. Milton, Byron, Shelley and Darwin were all rendered possible by this piece of good fortune. But there is no social system imaginable which will enable everybody to inherit a fortune, and in the society of the future, if exceptional individuals whose merit is not recognized while they are young are to be enabled to do their work, there must be definite institutions designed for this purpose. If this is not done, fundamental progress will cease, and men will tend to look back to the intellectual or artistic giants of former times as something beyond the capacity of the present age.

No society can be great without great individuals, and I should not think much of a world which had secured universal safety at the price of universal mediocrity. I think, however, that universal security, if it were attained by the kind of means that I have spoken of, would so much diminish envy and fear of eccentricity that the recognition, even in the young, of possible exceptional merit would not encounter the psychological resistance which it now has to meet in the great majority of mankind. If this is indeed the case, and if such institutions as I have spoken of can be established, the happy world that I am envisaging can be not only happy but glorious. I cannot believe that what is dark and dreadful and destructive in the souls of men is essential to the production of great works of imagination. I believe, on the contrary, that it lies within the power of man to create edifices of shining splendor, from which the glory and greatness of which human thought and feeling are capable shall spread a light unmixed with darkness, filling men's hearts with joy and their thoughts with clarity. Such a world is possible. It rests with men to choose whether they will create it, or allow the human race to perish in anger and sordid hate.

Man, in the long ages since he descended from the trees, has passed arduously and perilously through a vast dusty desert, surrounded by the whitening bones of those who have perished by the way, maddened by hunger and thirst, by fear of wild beasts, by dread of enemies, not only living enemies, but specters of dead rivals projected on to the dangerous world by the intensity of his own fears. At last he has emerged from the desert into a smiling land, but in the long night he has forgotten how to smile. We cannot believe in the brightness of the morning. We think it trivial and deceptive; we cling to old myths that allow us to go on living with fear and hate—above all, hate of ourselves, miserable sinners. This is folly. Man now needs for his salvation only one thing: to open his heart to joy, and leave fear to gibber through the glimmering darkness of a forgotten past. He must lift up his eyes and say: "No, I am not a miserable sinner; I am a being who, by a long and arduous road, have discovered how to make intelligence master natural obstacles, how to live in freedom and joy, at peace with myself and therefore with all mankind." This will happen if men will choose joy rather than sorrow. If not, eternal death will bury man in deserved oblivion.

ABOUT THE AUTHOR

BERTRAND ARTHUR WILLIAM RUSSELL *received the Nobel Prize for literature in 1950. He is the grandson of Lord John Russell, the British Foreign Secretary during the Civil War. Before going to Cambridge he was educated at home by governesses and tutors, acquiring a thorough knowledge of German and French; and it has been said that his "admirable and lucid English style may be attributed to the fact that he did not undergo a classical education at a public school." Certainly, this style is perceptible in the many books that have flowed from his pen during half a century—books that have shown him to be the most profound of mathematicians, the most brilliant of philosophers, and the most lucid of popularizers. His most recent major works are* A History of Western Philosophy, *published in 1945;* Human Knowledge: Its Scope and Limits, *published in 1948;* Authority and the Individual *published in 1949; and* Unpopular Essays, *that grossly mistitled book, published in 1951.*

901　　　　　R911

Russell　　　　　　　1.80

New hopes for a changing world